THE SONG OF ROLAND

THE LIBRARY OF LIBERAL ARTS
OSKAR PIEST, *Founder*

THE SONG OF ROLAND

TRANSLATED BY

PATRICIA TERRY

BARNARD COLLEGE

WITH AN INTRODUCTION

AND BIBLIOGRAPHY BY HAROLD MARCH

PROFESSOR EMERITUS OF FRENCH

SWARTHMORE COLLEGE

THE LIBRARY OF LIBERAL ARTS

PUBLISHED BY

Macmillan Publishing Company
New York
Collier Macmillan Publishers
London

For my mother
Sarah Press Blech
who set my course for France

and in memory of
Helen Carlson

TRANSLATOR'S PREFACE

Fidelity varies in kind and in degree. Poems insist that a translator be faithful in *their* fashion, which depends on the techniques they themselves embody for translating their author's intentions into art. The poet himself appears mainly in his defects, as if glimpsed through the small hole made by an imperfect or too-obvious rhyme, a misguided image. In the *Roland*, when he occasionally says "I," one is startled by a stranger.

Turoldus, however he may have lived, preferred fighting to contemplation, and placed the glory of France higher than that of poetry. I had assumed that his poem would do the same—that is, care more about the end than the means. But when I began the translation I was considerably surprised to find that each line seemed to defend the importance of its own stylistic details. Not so much as a repeated "and" ("and feet and fists and saddle-trees and spines") could be removed without legitimate protest. I hasten to say that these remarks will not lead to a claim that all the details of the *Roland* have been preserved by this translation. They are intended to appease my conscience, and to express the highest admiration for the craftsmanship which is second nature to the poem.

Certain literary qualities may be the result of either knowing calculation or an ignorance of possibilities. The *Roland's* unvaried, drumlike rhythm is monotonous, but it sweeps the reader along on its compelling current. The syntax is so simple that the least departure from the techniques of plain English prose seemed in the worst sense "poetical," because the final effect of this simplicity is grandeur. The vocabulary is equally strict in its avoidance of anything in the least elaborate, and whether or not this is due to the poet's preference, the poem rejects any over-sophisticated word, as a living organism expels a foreign body. The characteristic tone of the *Roland* might be explained by a certain modesty in the poet which made him instinctively throw away opportunities to be overly dramatic, or it may be credited to a conscious, and French, preference for understatement and laconic exaggeration. In either case the generally flat diction gives qualifying statements an intensity which they would not have had if the surrounding verses were too emphatic. When Turoldus says it was a beautiful evening, one feels it really must have been.

While a suitable vocabulary may quite readily be found in English, the rhythm presents a more complicated problem. No matter how carefully lines of verse may be constructed so that in syllable count and accentuation they imitate the meter of the *Roland*, the English-speaking reader, unaccustomed to a regular caesura, habitually fails to notice it. Then, instead of having four principal accents in each line, the meter tends to be distorted into a vague iambic pentameter; and if the hypnotic marching rhythm of the poem is lost, most of the power goes with it.

The best solution I could find was simply to indicate the caesura by an actual break in the line, which creates at least a sufficiently heavy stress on the preceding syllable if not a real pause. I have followed the *Roland* poet in his practice of placing this caesura occasionally after the sixth syllable [1] instead of the fourth, and of sometimes allowing one extra syllable, unaccented and uncounted, to come before it. The lines in this version, however, all end with an accented syllable. I hoped, by this device, to compensate for the lack of assonance which, even if less effective in English than in Old French, would still have been an asset. Unfortunately my attempts to reproduce it resulted in an

---

[1] Some examples of 6/4 lines are: "Un faldestoel i unt, fait tut d'or mer" (115); "Quan ço vos mandet Carles, ki France tient" (470); "E Blancandrins i vint, al canud peil" (503).

excessively complicated syntax and too many departures
from the actual expressions of the text. On the other hand,
I have tried to indicate that the *laisse* functions as a dramatic
unit by ending each one with a strong assonance or rhyme.
The mysterious letters *Aoi* look like some kind of excla-
mation. This may be, as Jenkins suggests, a musical crescendo.
I have left *Aoi* as it appears in the Oxford manuscript,
except where its position is very obviously a copyist's mistake.
It occurs most often at the end of a *laisse,* where the verses
regularly tend toward a dramatic conclusion.

Where proper names have a form familiar in English I
have used it: Marsile (not Marsïlie or Marsilions), Ganelon
(not Guenles, Guenes, or Guenlon), and in general I have
followed what seemed the simplest procedure in each case,
refraining, however reluctantly, from the possibility in Old
French of having two forms with differing numbers of syllables to designate a single character.

To consider the *Roland* in its broad outline can yield
satisfying observations about the relation of form and
content. The sweep of the action is clearly dependent on
the propulsive rhythm; the fact that this momentum is nevertheless segmented brings into focus one facet of the drama
at a time. The poem is enriched, however, by nuances which
owe nothing to its basic style and may even be obscured
by it. Sometimes these are practical details which immediately make their subject more real: Marsile goes into the
orchard to be out of the sun, Falsaron's forehead measures
a good six inches, Roland's sword slashes through the spine
of Chernuble's horse without looking for a joint. The affective
resonance of certain words influences the action: Blancandrin
evokes "clere Espagne la bele" for which sons will more
readily be sacrificed; Ganelon's speech in *laisse* XXXVI
suggests a contrast between Marsile's dignity and his probable
fate as Charlemagne's captive; the faintly sententious quality
in some of Oliver's remarks guarantees that our sympathies
will remain with Roland. Minute devices indicate emotion,
as when Charlemagne strokes or twists or pulls his beard.

Other details have a psychological significance which is left entirely to the reader's appreciation. Ganelon, "who'd rather not be there," drops the glove. He shows disrespect for Charlemagne only in the supreme crisis when his treason is about to be discovered. Roland, concentrating on the battle, realizes that Oliver is angry only when the latter withdraws his consent to a marriage between his sister, Alda, and Roland. When he looks back over his life from the hilltop where it ends, Roland remembers first the many lands he had conquered. Christians are right, and pagans are wrong; but Margariz is the most charming knight on either side, and Marsile, asking his men to help him sit up straight when Baligant comes in, receives our immediate sympathy. Roland's words of repentence are imprecise enough to leave his heroic stature untouched, and yet so convincing that he, who might well have sinned the same way again, can be carried off to heaven with angelic and human rejoicing.

Whether such effects were intuitive or deliberate, it seems impossible that Turoldus could have been unaware of them. Perhaps he was like those cathedral builders who carved beautiful faces into the shadows near the roof for the pleasure of angels and, as it happened, for enthusiasts with searchlights.

PATRICIA TERRY

CONTENTS

INTRODUCTION

1.

The *Chanson de Roland* and the twentieth-century English-speaking reader have more in common than might at first glance appear. The poem was written by a Norman; the language in which it was composed was brought to England by the invaders in 1066; there it became, and for three centuries remained, the literary and court language, and it furnished an important component of modern English. And as this language has become foreign to everyone, English can stake something of a claim as a substitute—not quite as good as modern French, but even there the kinship is largely a matter of etymologies perceptible only to the philologist; to the ordinary Frenchman of today the language is at least as foreign as Spanish or Italian.

The translator must meet the challenge of verse, and poetry is notoriously difficult, if not impossible, to translate. But a good deal depends on the intention of the original poet. If with Verlaine he sets music in the first place—"De la musique avant toute chose"—then we must admit that his frail verbal magic cannot survive the metamorphosis of translation; the best the translator can do is to dissolve it and recondense something more or less equivalent beyond. But then he becomes a poet in his own right, and the enterprise of making the original poem accessible has failed. But this delicate unexportable bouquet is mainly a quality of lyric verse. If the intent of the original poem is narrative, with lyricism reduced to a few descriptive passages, the problem becomes much simpler; for in this sort of verse the principal instrument is rhythm, which can be carried over more readily than musical tonalities. And this is the sort of poem we have in the Oxford manuscript—the famous Digby 23 of the Bodleian Library, the oldest and best version of the _Chanson de Roland_, and the basis of the present translation.

It is written in a series of _laisses_—bundles of verse averaging fourteen lines in length and "leashed" together by final assonances. The _laisse_ is normally an independent unit semantically, syntactically, and prosodically; its last line is usually set aside within its own unit and often has a sententious or summary character, like the final couplet in a Shakespearean sonnet or the last line of one by Heredia.

The verse is decasyllabic, with strong accents on the fourth and tenth syllables and a caesura (which in this translation has been indicated by a space) after the fourth. In a small number of instances the caesura comes after the sixth syllable, a variation that was later to become common. In either member of the verse thus divided, there may be an additional unaccented syllable (a feminine ending) not counting toward the total ten. Both at the caesura and at the end of the line there is a natural pause, called for by both sense and syntax.

The result of these dispositions is a movement by a series of explosions. Continuity is furnished by echoes, near-echoes, and _reprises_, which re-enforce the normal continuity of character and incident. These characteristics Patricia Terry has reproduced in her translation, with one important exception: she has replaced the single assonance of the original _laisse_ by an assonanced couplet at its close, and more often than not this couplet is also rhymed.

It is perfectly possible to construct an English translation in which a single assonance is used at the end of each line of a _laisse_—indeed, it has been done more than once—but only at a cost. The difficulty comes from the difference in the accentuation of the two languages. In French the accent falls on the last syllable of a word, or the last but one where there is a feminine ending. Since both masculine and feminine endings are used in the assonance, all words are available to the poet, subject only to the restriction of assonance. In English the stress has a recessive tendency, and many words, being accented on the penult or ante-penult, cannot furnish an accented final vowel for the as-sonance system. This reduces the number of words available, cramps the poet's vocabulary, and introduces monotony. Patricia Terry's change allows her greater scope and supple-ness, and also emphasizes the tendency, already present in the original, to mark the close of the *laisse*.

So much for the mechanics of verse, which is only the beginning; there is still the intangible but very real matter of atmosphere. The *Chanson* reflects the attitudes and emotions of its eleventh-century Norman author, and for a clue to the Norman character at the time of the Conquest, we can do no better than to turn to William of Malmesbury, who wrote of them early in the twelfth century: "They are a race inured to war, and can hardly live without it. . . ." Then, after further remarks irrelevant to our purpose, he continues:

> They revived, by their arrival, the observances of reli-gion, which were everywhere grown lifeless in England. You might see churches rise in every village, and monasteries in the towns and cities built after a style unknown before; you might behold the country flourish-ing with renovated rites. . . .

There we have it: war and religion, and in neither of these great consumers of energy are we much like our fore-runners. We have not, alas! outgrown war, but we pride ourselves on disapproving of it; two world wars and the approach of push-button warfare have stripped it of its false glamour. We have not quite outgrown religion either, but its state with us is more pre-Conquest English than Norman. The real queston is: Can we still respond to heroism, in battle or in faith?

Just how the poet contrives to create his atmosphere is something of a mystery. His simplicity, his limited vocabu-lary (the whole poem is built out of 1,744 words), his rapid, stylized place descriptions, contribute to the effect,

as does the thumping fourth-syllable accent recurring like
the cadence of marching feet. But there is more. We are
made to feel that good and evil are absolute, not relative,
that valor and loyalty and honor are realities, not mere words,
and that the unseen world is very close.

2.

The *Chanson de Roland* is elaborated from a kernel of
historic fact. Einhard, in his *Vita Caroli Magni* (written between 814 and 821), relates that Charlemagne in 778 made
an expedition into Spain and received the surrender of
various towns and castles. As he was returning through a
pass in the Pyrenees, his baggage train and rear guard were
ambushed and destroyed by Basques (Wascones) hiding in
thick woods on the mountain tops; the assailants then
scattered and disappeared. Among three notables mentioned
by name as having been killed in this disaster is one
Hruodlandus Brittannici limitis praefectus—Roland, prefect
of the Breton march.

Some three centuries after this scanty item of intelligence
there is in existence a finished work of art elaborating it.
Between the two—darkness.

No scholar believes that the *Chanson* derives directly from
Einhard, without intermediate steps: it contains too many
evidences of established traditions, both in form and in
subject matter, for such a supposition. Besides, there is
just a glimmer of light in the dark tunnel: an anonymous
Saxon poet, writing (in Latin) about the year 888, said that
"vernacular songs were celebrating with great praise" Pippin,
Charles, Theoderic, Charlemagne, and Lothar. There is no
mention of Roland; why should there be? The names (except
for Theoderic the Merovingian) are those of Carolingian
kings. Nevertheless, here is evidence that as early as the ninth
century Charlemagne, his ancestors, and his descendants
were becoming legendary.

Neither the author nor the date of the *Chanson* is known.

Interpreting the closing line of the manuscript ("Ci falt la geste, que Turoldus declinet") to mean "Here ends the history, for Turoldus is declining [in health]," Jenkins makes a plausible case for the authorship of the whole poem by Thorold of Envermeu, of the Benedictine Abbey at Le Bec. But *declinet* may mean "composed" or "recited," and *que* may be a relative pronoun instead of a conjunction, so that the final line may mean, "Here ends the story told by Turoldus." Moreover, Turoldus is not necessarily the author of the poem; he might be its source, or even the copyist. The externally recorded illness of Thorold of Envermeu, although timely, may be irrelevant.

If we knew that Jenkins was right about the author, it would help us to date the poem. But we don't, and other evidence, internal and external, is tenuous. Linguistic phenomena cannot bring us much closer than a century to the real date of composition, and even this rough approximation is offset by the ever-present problem of distinguishing between author and copyist. The most reliable forward limit is 1131, when the poem was translated into Latin and then into German. From there on back everything is conjectural.

William of Malmesbury wrote that before the Battle of Hastings in 1066 the "song of Roland" was begun in order to stimulate those who were about to fight. But even if we could be sure that the historian was not just inventing a picturesque detail, was this *cantilena Rollandi* the poem of the Oxford manuscript (which, incidentally, bears no title)?

Some have found satisfaction in observing that the battle of Roncevaux in the *Chanson* falls into three stages as does the historical battle of Zalaca in 1086, and that consequently the *Chanson* must have been written after that date. But does a battle, historical or legendary, require precedent in order to fall into three stages?

The confrontation of Christianity and Islam in the poem, the insistence on the rightness of the one and the wrongness of the other, and finally the heavy duty laid upon Charlemagne to continue to defend Christendom against the infidel—all this suggests to many scholars that the poem was written in the age of the Crusades, or possibly (since the poet seems poorly informed about the Levant) as propaganda for launching the first armed expedition of 1096. But the connection with the Crusades is at best dubious, since there was a crusading spirit, in the sense of Christian war against the infidel, in the wars of Charlemagne and of his grandfather Charles Martel against the Arabs in Spain, long before the officially numbered Crusades began.

Almost as inconclusive have been the long debates on the origin of the *chansons de geste*, of which the *Roland* is, not the first, but the earliest extant. Expert after expert advances, gazes into the dark well, sees the reflection of his own earnest scholarly face; he goes his way, and we are little the wiser. There are, however, two theories that call for more particular notice, not so much because of evidence marshaled (although this is impressive in the case of the second of the theories) as because of their relation to the twin ideals, apparent in the *Chanson*, of the warrior and of the saint.

In 1812 the German poet Uhland described the *chanson de geste* as "the Germanic spirit in a Romanic form." The formula found such favor that it dominated nineteenth-century criticism in the field. It finally lost ground by being associated with the now thoroughly discredited *cantilena* theory: the idea that short popular songs, contemporary with the events narrated, sprang up "spontaneously" and were later patched together by jongleurs.

A century after Uhland's pronouncement, Joseph Bédier attacked his position, claiming that there was no real evidence of the descent of the *chanson de geste* from the Germanic epic, and that, on the contrary, it was a French creation of the age of the Crusades. Sanctuaries clustered around the great pilgrimage routes, and here local legends about heroes of the past were collected by monks and relayed to the pilgrims. In this way were disseminated materials for lives of secular notables, on the model of vernacular lives of the saints.

Bédier made a strong case but he did not succeed in banishing the "Germanic spirit" from the *Chanson*—if by that phrase we mean the glorification of carnage. There is already a traditional air about the warlike materials: the *gab* (the boast of future prowess), the enumeration of the hosts, the jeweled helmets and shields, the single combat, the pause for discussion followed by a resumption of combat, the mighty blow, the taunt over the fallen foe, the compliment from brothers-in-arms. Roland, aided by the relics in the hilt of his sword Durendal, specializes in the downstroke through helmet, skull, body, saddle and horse's back; this operation is performed three times by him (*laisses* CIV, CXIX, CXXIV) and once by Oliver (*laisse* CVII), who, though just as brave as Roland, went in for brains more than brawn; besides, his sword had fewer relics than Roland's. Some of the warlike materials are in the epic tradition extending back into classical antiquity, but the surgical details are not: entrails or broken spine protruding (lines 1201, 2247), the bared viscera (line 1278), brains bubbling down over forehead (line 2248). These matters are not for the squeamish, but the poet seems to be enjoying himself, as no doubt did the early hearers of his chanted lines.

It is a far cry from Saint Alexis, whose grand achievement was his long sojourn under the stairs of his father's house, unrecognized, and his unprotesting reception of the slops cast on his head, to the mighty Roland, at the mere sight of whom the pagan Grandoine, victor over several of the peers, trembles and tries to escape—unsuccessfully, of course. And if it seems strange for a priest or monk to relish these bloody deeds, we must remember his creation Archbishop Turpin:

> No tonsured priest who ever sang a mass
> Had such high courage to do heroic deeds. (1607–8)

Then rides forward the Saracen Abisme ("Abyss"—sink of iniquity):

> The fiercest man   in all that company.
> Evil at heart,   and guilty of great crimes,
> He has no faith   in Mary's holy Son.
> . . . .
> Archbishop Turpin   will be no friend to him—
> Seeing this pagan,   he longs to strike him down.
> In a low voice   he speaks thus to himself:
> "This man must be   a mighty heretic—
> Surely his death   has been too long delayed.
> I have no love   for men who are afraid." (1471–86)

The archbishop disposes of the dreadful Abisme in short order:

> Right through that pagan   his spear thrusts like a spit;
> He throws the body   into an empty space. (1505–6)

The fusion of warrior and priest that we see in Turpin is characteristic of the whole poem. Unlike *Beowulf*, which is a heathen poem with incongruous Christian insertions, the *Chanson de Roland* is basically and throughout a Christian work. Its subject is war against the enemies of God; its animating virtue, heroism. With this ideal and in such a cause, no shadow of doubt or whisper of scruple disturbs the poet's Christian serenity.

Bédier is convincing in his demonstration of the contribution of monastic legend and Christian atmosphere to the *chansons de geste*. It is true too that the *Vie de Saint Alexis* (as a sample of vernacular hagiography) is written in assonanced stanzas and decasyllabic lines, like the later *Chanson de Roland*. And when we have said so much, what have we done but repeat Uhland's formula in slightly different words?

Indeed, the "Romanic form" of that formula can be extended beyond the mere discipline of the assonance and the decasyllabic line: it may stand for the curbing by Latin Christendom of the northern tribes' lust for war.

3.

At the time of the historical battle of Roncevaux Charlemagne was a mere thirty-six years of age. "The mighty
Charles," who is onstage at the opening of the *Chanson*, is
greatly changed. His beard is now long and white (as how
should it not be after three hundred years?) and he is
given to stroking it in meditation or pulling it in vexation.
He sits under a pine tree and listens to the squabbles of
his knights. For fighting he now chiefly depends on his
nephew Roland (a promotion for Hruodlandus the prefect),
who brings him kings' crowns like so many bright red apples.

Charlemagne's role is uncomfortably dual. On the one
hand is God, whose viceroy on earth he is; on the other,
the barons of France—

> . . . for what he must decide
> The men of France   would always be his guide. (166–67)

Kings have sought counsel since the beginning of history,
but how they have taken it is another matter. Unlike the
pagan kings, who rule by infernal right and ask counsel in
the expectation of servile acquiescence, Charlemagne feels
obligated to respect the opinions of the majority—at least
the majority of an oligarchy, the barons of France. He does
so even against his better judgment, as in the embassy of
Ganelon, and the command of the rear guard.

His better judgment, we say; but it is really God's judgment. For angels stand by to help with messages from on
high, delivered by dream, or portent, or intuition, and it is
his unhappy destiny to attempt to conciliate God's will with
democratic process.

For the modern reader one of the merits of the *Chanson*
is that its characters are not all of a piece. Charlemagne is
not at ease in his imperial splendor; Ganelon the traitor
has courage, and up to a point he is a loyal vassal of Charle-

magne, though his hatred of Roland leads him into rationalizing treachery. Heroism in the enemy is given its due, and the poet permits himself regret that certain brave pagans are not baptized.

Roland, the hero of the poem, on early acquaintance seems naïve, but eventually he turns out to be the most significantly complex of the characters. He is brave, certainly, but so is Oliver, so are all the peers. His special superiority comes from a kind of ecstasy in battle, a furious self-abandon in onslaught that nothing can stop, and from a tremendous pride in his country, his lineage, and most of all in his own fair name. His impetuosity and his pride make enemies for him and are responsible for the tragic mistake that leads to his death: his refusal to summon aid in time.

Oliver too can perform prodigious feats in the heat of battle, but for him fighting is not an end in itself. His prime duty, as he sees it, is to win battles for his emperor, not to exalt his personal prestige. Courage without prudence is of little worth. So it is symbolically right that it should be he who climbs to the hilltop and warns of the approach of the Saracens. Three times he urges Roland to sound his horn and three times Roland refuses. Oliver says no more, but prepares to play his part with fortitude. Only when the heaps of the needlessly slain bear visible witness to Roland's presumptuous folly does he break out in reproaches and withdraw his consent to the marriage of his sister, Alda, with Roland.

But there is another side to Roland: a gentleness, a humility, a courtesy, to offset his faults of violence. This quality has been there all along, but submerged; it accounts for the love of his followers as much as his prowess—or rather it is the striking combination of the two that commands their devotion. In the extremity of danger Roland's gentleness comes out beside his courage:

Fair to behold,   he laughs, serene and gay.
Now close behind him   comes Oliver, his friend,
With all the Frenchmen   cheering their mighty lord.

Fiercely his eyes   confront the Saracens;
Humbly and gently   he gazes at the Franks,
Speaking to them   with gallant courtesy: (1159–64)

In the end it is this nobler Roland that is dominant. Not that he gives up violence—he remains a warrior to the end, and moments before his death he wakes from a swoon to kill one last Saracen, this time with a blow from his oliphant. What he surrenders is his pride, by which he caused the death of the flower of Charlemagne's army:

Barons of France,   because of me you die;
I can't protect you,   I cannot keep you safe:
Look now to God   who never failed a trust. (1863–65)

The three mighty blasts of Roland's oliphant, echoing through thirty leagues of mountain pass, proclaim his admission of error. Follow more blows given and taken, a last weakening summons of the horn, the answering crash of Charlemagne's sixty thousand trumpets as the avenging host returns. There are the deaths, the commendations, the epitaphs. Oliver, reconciled with Roland, calls blessings on his head and falls. The great archbishop dies in a last effort to bring water to Roland:

Turpin is dead   who fought for Charlemagne.
With mighty blows,   with wise and holy words,
Against the pagans   he championed the Faith.
May God in heaven   bless him and grant him grace.
(2242–45)

Roland is the last. Without earthly commendation,

Roland, in homage,   offers his glove to God.
Saint Gabriel comes   and takes it from his hand.
(2389–90)

So dies the great warrior and so, accompanied by flights of angels, is redeemed his better part.

4.

The bloody field of Roncevaux, the tremendous blows, the loyal constancy of brothers-in-arms—all this is a man's world. Women are the reward of victory; they wait in sweet France

or heathen Saragossa for the return of their bloodstained
heroes. In neither country are they very highly esteemed;
where heroism is in the ascendant, soft beauty is depreciated.
Perhaps a woman fares a little worse among the pagans, if
we may judge by Clarien's contemptuous silencing of the
lamentations of Queen Bramimonde: "Lady, don't talk so
much!" (2724)

There are two women in the *Chanson*: Bramimonde the
pagan and Alda the Christian. Their roles are brief but
significant.

Bramimonde is notable chiefly for her inconstancy. From
gods and men she expects prompt service. Life owes her
a man in good condition, and the gods owe him victory in
battle. When her husband Marsile, having been promised the
life of Roland, the Emperor's right hand, returns defeated,
with his own right hand symbolically amputated by this
same Roland, she reviles and dishonors the images of her
gods. For her husband she weeps and laments, but she
considers him dead already; and indeed his end is not long
delayed. Meanwhile a man dishonored and maimed is not
good enough for her, and she abruptly starts praising
Charlemagne and the Franks (*laisses* CLXXXVII and
CLXXXVIII). Consciously or unconsciously she is getting
ready for conversion to Christianity, and who can doubt
that beyond the limits of the *Chanson* a new husband awaits
the queen, newly baptized as Juliana? Charlemagne has commanded that she be converted "by love," and though the
word doubtless denotes Christian Charity rather than Eros,
with women like Bramimonde a little ambiguity is permissible.

Alda is an altogether different sort of woman. When
Charlemagne returns to Aix she marches straight up to him
and demands, "Where is Roland?" Charlemagne, weeping,
pulling his beard, replies:

"Sister, sweet friend,   I can't bring back the dead . . ."

He promises to give her Louis, his son and heir. But—

> Alda replies, "Your words seem to me strange.
> The saints and angels, and God above forbid
> That I live on when Roland has been slain!"
> Her color fades, she falls down at Charles' feet,
> And dies—may God have mercy on her soul. (3717–21)

Charlemagne thinks she has merely fainted, as the Franks are given to doing; he himself fainted at sight of Roland's body, and one hundred thousand Frenchmen, with earth-shaking unanimity, followed his example. But Alda is really dead.

Here is something new, something quite beyond the range of a greedy Bramimonde. Could it be romantic love, that strange passion whose nature it is to overshoot its mark, whose desire is like the love of God—and of death? At the end of the eleventh century, where at least in spirit the *Chanson* belongs, the troubadours were already writing, beginning to build a body of literature now sensual, now courtly and chivalric, now rarefied into love of the *princesse lointaine*. From these attitudes grew the romances of the Arthurian cycle that were presently to sweep Europe. From this matter were shaped Laura, and the heavenly Beatrice. Because the chief poets were men, the romantic ideal was embodied in the figure of a woman. Like the Virgin she stood in her niche and received homage, but she did not step down and die for love. Elaine of later romance, who died for the love of Launcelot, remains an exception. There is nothing deeply moving about her story. Her epitaph might have been, "Poor child—silly child."

But these are early days. Despite the majestic beard of Charlemagne, the spirit of the *Chanson* is inescapably young. It is best expressed by young Roland (he could only be young)—serene, gay, flaunting his white banner, prancing on Veillantif before his cheering men. This man would never die for the love of Alda, but she could die for him. In her constancy and in his courtesy lie the seeds of future romance, but now we are in the heroic age. This is the medieval morning.

5.

From the opening of the poem we have realized that the war is not just between Frank and Saracen, but also between God and the pagan divinities, who are evil and false but who share with God a certain supernatural reality. In the first instance the issue must be decided on the purely human plane, but the supernatural is attentive to what is going on, never too far away.

As the battle in the pass moves toward its inevitable end, a great storm strikes France:

> Through rushing winds   long peals of thunder roar,
> And heavy rains,   enormous hailstones fall,
> Great bolts of lightning   are striking everywhere.
> Now the whole earth   is trembling dreadfully
> From Saint Michel   all the way down to Seinz,
> From Besançon   to Wissant on the sea;
> There is no stronghold   without a shattered wall.
> At noontime shadows   darken the light of day;
>
> . . . .
>
> Many declare,   "The world is at an end—
> The Day of Wrath   has come upon us now!"
> But they know nothing,   and they believe a lie.
> The heavens grieve   that Roland is to die. (1424–37)

This darkness at noon (a Biblical supernatural, like the subsequent stopping of the sun) foreshadows the temporary triumph of evil. Then come the three blasts on the oliphant. Roland has always considered this mighty horn as reserved for special occasions, Ganelon's lie to the contrary notwithstanding. To Charlemagne it now speaks with no uncertain voice: Roland is fighting and he needs help. Roland himself, well knowing that help cannot arrive in time, is confessing his fault and calling for a Christian burial. And perhaps Gabriel, the angel of the Annunciation and of the Last Day, is particularly alert to the sound of the trumpet, for now he moves in more closely. He takes personal charge of Charlemagne's dreams, stands guard by his bed at night, and whispers encouragement in his ear at a crucial moment in the battle with Baligant.

Some critics have felt that the Baligant episode is redundant. Why not limit the story to the treason of Ganelon, the battle of Roncevaux, the extermination of Marsile's army, and the judgment of the traitor?

And so indeed the poet might have done, had his only concern been the story line. But with the Baligant episode a different dimension is introduced: metaphysical good and evil are at grips. Marsile has not the stature needed for what is to come. When he loses his right hand he collapses, whereas Charlemagne, deprived of his metaphorical right hand, Roland, rises to new heights.

Baligant is a worthy foe. He is no grotesque grinning devil, but beautiful as a fallen angel:

As for his courage, he's proved it many times.
God! What a hero if he had been baptized! (3163–64)

It is not by chance that his spear, mighty as the one carried by Goliath of Gath, is named Evil, nor that in the hilt of Charlemagne's sword is mounted the spearhead that wounded the side of Christ: Baligant is the spearhead of Evil, and against him is ranged the Passion of Christ. On both sides the beards are long and snowy white, for the Ancient of Days is both Good and Evil.

To the trumpeting of the oliphant the stage enlarges, and we see that the action we have been following is suspended between Heaven and Hell; the actors are moved from above and from below.

Baligant challenges, Charlemagne accepts:

"Barons of France, take up your arms and ride!" (2986)

So too behind their dragon-standard the pagans ride, with Baligant showing the way:

He shakes his spear, to make his meaning plain,
And holds it high, the point toward Charlemagne.
(3327–28)

Led by the long white beards whipping in the wind, the two armies rush together. "And there was war in heaven," records the Book of Revelation: "Michael and his angels fought against the dragon; and the dragon fought and his angels, and prevailed not; neither was their place found any more in heaven."

Or as "Turoldus" (whoever he may be) sums it up:

The pagans flee,   for that is what God wills. (3625)

But the respite is temporary, for presently Saint Gabriel, with the voice of the prophets of old, summons Charlemagne to a new war.

"God!" says the king,   "how weary is my life!" (4000)

He gives his beard one last pull, Turoldus "declines," and the lights go out.

There is something grim about the pass at Roncevaux:

High are the hills,   deep valleys shun the light;
The cliffs rise grey,   the gorges hold dark fear. (814–15)

Here Evil treacherously assaulted, and Good for a time went down. Here echoed Roland's horn, as down the years it echoes still.

And if the battle still goes on, why that too is as God wills.

HAROLD MARCH

SELECTED BIBLIOGRAPHY

Basic Books

La chanson de Roland: reproduction phototypique du manuscrit Digby 23 de la Bodleian Library d'Oxford. Paris: Société des anciens textes français, 1933.

Les textes de la Chanson de Roland. 10 volumes. Paris: Éditions de la geste Francor, 1940–44.

La Chanson de Roland, Oxford version. Edited by T. ATKINSON JENKINS New York: D. C. Heath & Co., 1929.

La chanson de Roland, publiée d'après le manuscrit d'Oxford et traduite par Joseph Bédier. Paris: L'Édition d'art H. Piazza, 1922.

La chanson de Roland, commentée par Joseph Bédier. Paris: L'Édition d'art H. Piazza, 1927.

BÉDIER, JOSEPH. *Les légendes épiques: Recherches sur la formation des chansons de geste.* Paris: Champion, 1908–13; 2nd edn., 1914–21; 3rd edn., 1926–29.

Bibliography

CABEEN, D. C., general editor. *A Critical Bibliography of French Literature.* Volume I: *The Medieval Period.* Edited by URBAN T. HOLMES, JR. Syracuse: Syracuse University Press, 1947.

Anthologies

STUDER, PAUL, and WALTERS, E. G. R., editors. *Historical French Reader, Medieval Period.* Oxford: The Clarendon Press, 1924.

PAUPHILET, ALBERT, editor. *Poètes et romanciers du moyen âge.* "Bibliothèque de la Pléiade." Paris: Gallimard, 1952.

ROSS, JAMES BRUCE, and McLAUGHLIN, MARY MARTIN, editors. *The Portable Medieval Reader.* New York: The Viking Press, 1949.

General

ADAMS, HENRY. *Mont-Saint-Michel and Chartres.* Boston and New York: Houghton Mifflin Company, 1905, 1933.

DAWSON, CHRISTOPHER. *Medieval Essays.* New York: Image Books, 1959.

SAULNIER, VERDUN-L. *La littérature française du moyen âge.* Paris: Presses Universitaires de France, 1948.

NOTE ON THE TEXT

This translation is based on the Oxford manuscript as edited by Joseph Bédier (Paris: L'Édition d'art H. Piazza, 1960). Any variants used are from the edition of T. Atkinson Jenkins (Boston: D. C. Heath and Co., 1929), and are indicated in the notes. References to "V⁴" in the notes designate the "Venice IV" manuscript of the Library of St. Mark at Venice, printed by Eugene Kölbing, 1877.

THE SONG OF ROLAND

THE SONG OF ROLAND

I

The mighty Charles,   our emperor and king,
Seven long years   has been at war in Spain;
That lofty land   lies conquered to the sea.
No fortress now   is standing in his way,
No walls, no towns   remain for him to break,
Except for Saragossa,   high on its hill,
Ruled by Marsile,   who has no love for God;
He serves Apollo,   and to Mohammed prays—
But he will come,   and soon, to evil days! AOI

II

In Saragossa,   the pagan king, Marsile,   10
Walks through an orchard   whose trees give cooling shade.
The king reclines   on a blue marble bench;

8. The gods of the Saracens are Apollin, Mahumet, and Tervagant.
The origins of the first two are obvious, but it should be understood
that as they are conceived by the *Roland* poet the one was no more
appropriate to the Mohammedans than the other. As for Tervagan, or
Tervagant, even his source is obscure. The Saracens in the poem
worship idols, and although the laws of their gods are written down
in a book, this would indicate at best a very faint awareness of the
Koran.
12. I have translated *bloi* throughout as "blue," but Jenkins' "yellow"
is also possible. Professor March has suggested that the two etymons
responsible for the confusion may have been the Old North Frankish
blaud, meaning yellow, and the Germanic *blaw*, meaning blue.

3

His host assembles, some twenty thousand men.
He speaks these words to all his dukes and counts:
"Now hear, my lords, what evils weigh us down!
For Charles has come, the ruler of sweet France,
To seize our lands, and bring us to our knees.
I have no army to fight against his own;
No men of mine will drive him to defeat—
20 Give me your counsel, as you are true and wise,
Save me from death, and from this bitter shame."
Mute are the pagans, except for one alone:
Blancandrin speaks, whose castle is Val-Fonde.

III

Among the pagans Blancandrin was wise,
A trusted vassal, a brave and loyal knight,
Clever enough to think of good advice.
He tells the king, "You need not be afraid.
Send word to Charles, the arrogant, the proud,
That you in friendship salute him as your lord,
30 Offer him gifts: bears and lions and dogs,
And seven hundred camels, a thousand hawks,
Four hundred mule-loads of silver and of gold,
And fifty carts to form a wagon-train.
He'll have enough to pay his hired men.
He has campaigned so long here in this land,
He won't refuse to go back home to Aix.
Say you will meet him in France, on Michael's Day,
To be converted, adopt the Christian law,
And do him homage in friendship and good will.
40 If hostages are needed, say you will send

16. The adjective is so nearly part of the noun that even the Saracens
speak of *dolce France.*
24. In the *laisses similaires* which occur at several of the poem's most
dramatic moments, the action is suspended while the content of a *laisse*
is restated with a different assonance. The point of view is somewhat
altered, and the emotion intensified.
31. Mewed—that is, adult—hawks.
36. Aix la Chapelle.

Ten, even twenty, to witness your good faith:
We'll have to yield the sons our wives have borne—
The risk is death, but I will send my own.
Better that they should sacrifice their heads
Than that we lose our honor and our pride,
And live as beggars with all our rights denied!" AOI

IV

Says Blancandrin, "I swear by my right hand,
And by this beard that ripples on my chest,
You'll see the French disband their troops and go,
The Franks will soon be on their way to France.   50
And when each one has found his home again,
Charles, in the chapel that he has built in Aix,
Will give a feast in honor of the saint,
On Michael's Day, when we'll have sworn to come—
But of our coming the French will see no sign.
The king is proud, and cruel is his heart;
He'll have the heads of all our men cut off.
But better far that they should lose their heads
Than that we lose this shining land, fair Spain,
And be condemned to hardship and disgrace."   60
The pagans say, "That may well be the case!"

V

The king declared the council at an end.
He summoned forth Clarin of Balaguer,
Estramariz, and Eudropin his peer,

---

50. The "Franks" (*Francs*) and "French" (*Françeis*) are for the most
part used as synonymous terms. Occasionally, however, the Franks of
France are distinguished from the Franks from elsewhere in the Empire.
It is stated that Charles prefers the men of France to all others (3031);
in 3976-77 the bishops of France are mentioned separately from those of
Bavaria and Germany. The boundaries of "France" are also variable,
sometimes including the whole of Charlemagne's empire (larger than
life), sometimes more restricted.

Long-bearded Guarlan,   and with him Priamon,
And Machiner,   his uncle Maheu,
And Joüner,   Malbien d'Oltremer,
And Blancandrin,   to be his embassy;
These ten he chose   from his most evil men.
70 "Barons, my lords,   you'll go to Charlemagne,
He is in Cordres,   holding the town besieged.
The olive branch   you'll carry in your hands,
A sign of peace   and your humility.
If you are clever,   if you persuade the king,
Much gold and silver   shall be your thanks from me,
Fiefdoms and land,   as much as you desire."
The pagans say,   "That's more than we require."   AOI

VI

Then King Marsile   declares the council closed.
He tells his men,   "Thus you shall go, my lords:
80 Hold in your hands   the olive branch of peace,
And speak for me   to Charlemagne the king;
In his God's name,   ask him to grant me grace.
Say that before   a single month has passed,
I'll bring to France   a thousand of my men,
There be converted,   adopt the Christian law,
Become his vassal   in loyalty and love.
For this he'll have   what hostages he will."
Says Blancandrin,   "Our wishes he'll fulfill."   AOI

VII

The ten white mules   are brought for them to ride;
90 Suatilie's king   had sent them to Marsile.

71. "Cordres" suggests Cordova, but that city would then be in northern
Spain. I have generally preferred to copy the version of the name as
it appears in Bédier's translation. The poet's notions of geography are
more flamboyant than accurate, and no more than a general effect can
be derived from them. The same applies to the names of the more
exotic peoples, especially among Baligant's pagans.

Their reins are gold,   their saddles silver-trimmed.
The envoys mount,   and as they ride away,
Each in his hand   holds high the olive branch.
They go to Charles,   who rules the Frankish land;
He will not see   the treachery they've planned.   AOI

VIII

The Emperor Charles   is jubilant and gay:
The lofty walls   of Cordres are torn down,
His catapults   have laid its towers low;
His knights rejoice,   for great is their reward—
Silver and gold,   and costly gear for war.   *100*
In all the city   no pagan now remains
Who isn't dead   or one of the true Faith.
In a great orchard,   Charlemagne sits in state.
With him are Roland,   and Oliver, his friend;
A duke called Samson,   and fiery Anseïs,
Geoffroy of Anjou,   flag-bearer for the king;
The two companions   Gerin and Gerier.
And with these barons   is no small group of men,
For fifteen thousand   came with them from sweet France.
The knights are seated   on carpets of white silk;   *110*
The older men,   or clever, pass the time
Playing backgammon,   or else they sit at chess;
The nimble youths   prefer to fence with swords.
Beneath a pine,   beside a briar-rose,
A throne is placed—   it's made of purest gold.
There sits the king,   the ruler of sweet France;
White is his beard,   and silver streaks his hair,
Handsome his form,   his bearing very proud:
No stranger needs   to have him pointed out.
The Saracens   dismount and come on foot   *120*
To greet the king,   as friendly envoys would.

---

106. Geoffroy of Anjou is the king's *gunfanuner*, the bearer of the
gonfalon, or battle flag.

IX

Then Blancandrin   begins to make his speech.
He says to Charles,   "May God grant you His grace,
That glorious Lord   to whom all men must pray!
We've come to you   at King Marsile's command;
He's learned about the law   that saves men's souls,
And of his wealth   he wants to offer you
Lions and bears,   and leash-trained hunting dogs,
And seven hundred camels,   a thousand hawks,
130   Silver and gold   four hundred mules will bear,
And fifty carts   to form a wagon-train.
These will be loaded   with silver coins and gold,
Enough for you   to well reward your men.
You have campaigned   so long here in this land,
It must be time   to go back home to Aix;
My lord Marsile   says he will follow you."
The Emperor Charles   holds both hands up toward God;
He bows his head,   and gives himself to thought.   AOI

X

The Emperor Charles   sits with his head bent low.
140   He was not known   for answering in haste:
Always he liked   to take his time to speak.   *Verbal*
When he looked up,   his face was stern and proud.
Thus he replies: "You've spoken well indeed.
But King Marsile   has been no friend of mine;
Of what you say,   although your words are fair,
How shall I know   how much I can believe?"
"Take hostages,"   the Saracen replies,
"Ten or fifteen   or twenty you shall have;

140. The shifts of tense in the *Roland* sometimes seem to provide
dramatic emphasis by bringing an action closer to the reader, but
often have no apparent purpose. I have followed them whenever such
accuracy was not obtrusive.

Though he risks death,   I'll send a son of mine,
And there will be   some even nobler men.   150
When, in your palace   at Aix, you hold the feast
That celebrates   Saint Michael of the Sea,
My lord Marsile   declares that he will come,
And, in those baths   which were God's gift to you,
He will be baptized,   adopt the Christian faith."
Then answers Charles,   "It still is not too late."   AOI

XI

Fair was the evening,   the sun set pure of cloud.
By Charles' command   the mules were led to stalls.
In the great orchard   he had a tent set up,
And there he lodged   the envoys of Marsile;   160
Twelve of his servants   attended to their needs.
There they remained   until it was bright day.
When, in the morning,   the emperor arose,
He heard a mass   and matins first of all,
And then the king   sat down beneath a pine,
And called his barons: for what he must decide
The men of France   would always be his guide.   AOI

XII

Beneath a pine   the emperor takes his place,
And calls his barons   to say what they would do.
Duke Ogier,   Archbishop Turpin came,   170
Richard the Old,   his nephew called Henri,

152. Saint Michael, patron of Mont-Saint-Michel.
154. The mineral springs and baths at Aix, or, as Jenkins suggests, the
buildings connected with them in which the ceremony of baptism would
take place. Their supernatural origin is not mentioned by Einhard, but
many such divine contributions embellished the personality of
Charlemagne.
161. The word in the text is *serjanz*, usually translated as "sergeants."
They apparently function, however, as personal attendants of the
higher-ranking knights.

From Gascony   the brave Count Acelin,
Thibaut of Reims,   his cousin Count Milon,
And there were both   Gerin and Gerier—
Count Roland came,   together with these two,
And Oliver,   so noble and so brave;
The Franks of France,   more than a thousand men.
Ganelon came   by whom they were betrayed.
And then began   the talks that evil swayed.   AOI

XIII

180   "Barons, my lords,"   says Charles the Emperor,
"This I have heard   from envoys of Marsile:
Of his great wealth   he'll send me a good part,
Lions and bears,   and leash-trained hunting dogs,
Seven hundred camels,   a thousand hawks,
Four hundred mule-loads   of fine Arabian gold,
And with these gifts,   some fifty heavy carts.
But he requests   that I return to France,
And says that when   I'm home again in Aix,
He'll come and yield   to holy Christian law,
190   He'll take the Faith,   and hold his lands from me;
But I don't know   the secrets of his heart."
"We must think twice,"   they say, "before we start!"   AOI

XIV

The king has brought   his discourse to an end.
And now Count Roland   has risen to his feet;
He speaks his mind   against the Saracens,
Saying to Charles,   "You can't believe Marsile!
It's seven years   since first we came to Spain;
For you I've conquered   Noples and Commibles,
I took Val-Terre   and all the land of Pine,
200   And Balaguer,   Tudela, Sedilie.
There King Marsile   displayed his treachery:
Of his vile pagans   he sent to you fifteen;

Each in his hand   held high the olive branch,
And when they spoke,   we heard this very speech.
You let your Franks   decide what should be done;
The plan they chose   was foolishness indeed:
You sent two counts   as envoys to the king,
Basant was one,   the other was Basile—
They left their heads   on a hill near Haltilies!
Finish the fight   the way it was begun: *210*
To Saragossa   lead on your gathered host,
Though all your life   at war here you remain,
Avenge those men   so villainously slain!" AOI

XV

The Emperor Charles   has kept his head bowed down;
He strokes his beard,   arranges his moustache,
And to his nephew   says neither yes nor no.
The French are silent,   except for Ganelon;
He stands up straight   and comes before the king,
With wrathful pride   begins his argument,
Saying to Charles: "Believe no underling,   *220*
Not me, not Roland,   who speaks against your good!

220. Ganelon's first words, *Ja mar crerez bricun*, echo Roland's *Ja mar crerez Marsilie!* (196), and this would seem to indicate immediately the basic motivation of his argument. Probably Ganelon does believe that Marsile's offer should be accepted, but his main interest is in seizing the chance of effectively opposing Roland at a time when the latter's excessive pride has been made obvious to all. Very likely Ganelon had not considered the possibility of being made ambassador to Marsile, and the unpleasantness of this surprise accounts for his violent reaction in *laisse* XX. That he was not a coward is well demonstrated elsewhere.

Just why Ganelon so hates Roland is not known to us; it may have been to the poet's contemporaries. The explanation Ganelon gives toward the end of the poem (3758), that Roland had cheated him of gold and possessions, seems insufficient, or at least unsatisfying. A heroic stepson might well inspire a particularly virulent jealousy, all the more acute in that it would have to be, in the case of Charlemagne's nephew, quite well concealed.

When King Marsile   sends messengers to say
He'll place his hands in yours,   and be your man,
He'll do you homage   for all the lands of Spain,
And he'll observe   our holy Christian law—
Whoever urges you   to scorn this peace
Does not care, Sire,   what kind of death we die.
A man too proud   will recklessly advise;
Let's heed no fools,   and keep to what is wise!"   AOI

XVI

230   When he had stopped,   Duke Naimon rose to speak;
In all the court   there was no better man.
He said to Charles,   "You've heard Count Ganelon;
I think the answer   that he has given you
Contains good sense,   if it be understood.
For King Marsile   there's no hope in this war:
All of his castles   have fallen to your hands,
Your catapults   have broken down his walls,
His towns are burned,   his men brought to defeat.
Now envoys ask   your mercy for the king—
240   If we refuse,   we're guilty of grave sin.
Since hostages will prove   he did not lie,
In this great war   there's no one left to fight."
The Frenchmen say,   "The duke is in the right!"

XVII

"Barons, my lords,   which one of you shall go
To Saragossa,   to talk with King Marsile?"
Duke Naimon says,   "I'll do it, by your leave.

234. Jenkins understands the line to mean "provided that it [Ganelon's counsel] be properly understood." He feels that Ganelon's meaning was obscured by his emotions. The speech seems to me clear enough, but Naimon's restatement is certainly more objective. Bédier's reading, "You have only to do what he says," seems less likely and harder to defend. 246. Roland has sometimes been criticized for not being the first to offer to go. But Naimon, who approved Ganelon's speech, would have to volunteer immediately.

Yield to me now   the envoy's staff and glove."
Answers the king,   "The wisest of my men!
By this white beard,   by my moustache I swear
So far from me   I'll never let you go.   *250*
Sit down; if you are wanted,   I'll let you know!"

XVIII

"Barons, my lords,   what envoy can we send
To Saragossa,   held by the Saracen?"
Count Roland says,   "Let me talk to Marsile!"
"No, you shall not!"   Count Oliver replies,
"Your heart is fierce,   and you are quick to wrath—
If you are sent,   there's sure to be a fight.
By the king's leave,   I'll be the one to go."
Answers the king,   "Be quiet, both of you!
Not you nor he   will set foot in that town!   *260*
And by this beard   that you can see is white,
I'll tell you now   the twelve peers all must stay."
The French are silent;   they dare not disobey.

XIX

Turpin of Reims   has risen from his place.
He says to Charles,   "Leave all your Franks in peace.
For seven years   you've been here in this land
Where you have suffered   great hardships and fatigue.
Give, Sire, to me   the envoy's staff and glove,
And I will seek   the Spanish Saracen;
I would be glad   to know what he is like."   *270*
But much displeased   the emperor replies,
"I'll hear no more—   go to your place and sit.
Keep your advice   until I ask for it!" AOI

XX

"My valiant knights,"   says Charles the Emperor,
"Choose for me now   the nobleman of France

Who is to take   my message to Marsile."
"I name," says Roland,   "Stepfather Ganelon."
The Franks reply,   "He'd do it very well;
We could not make   a wiser choice than this."
280 Count Ganelon   is furious indeed;
Casting aside   his cloak of marten furs,
He shows a tunic   made of the finest silk.
Steel-grey his eyes   and very proud his face,
His carriage noble,   his chest is large around;
He looks so handsome,   his peers all turn and stare.
He says, "You fool,   rash are your words, and wild.
Everyone knows   I'm stepfather to you,
Yet you name me   the envoy to Marsile!
If God should grant   that I come home again,
290 I won't forget—   and you'll face such a feud
That it will last   as long as you're alive!"
"I hear," says Roland,   "your foolishness and pride.
Everyone knows   I answer threats with scorn;
A man of wisdom   this embassy requires—
I'll take your place,   if the king so desires." AOI

XXI

Ganelon says,   "You shall not take my place!
You're not my man,   nor am I your liege-lord.
But Charles commands me   to serve him in this way:
In Saragossa   I'll talk to King Marsile.
300 But I will find   some little trick to play,
Fit to relieve   my fury at this wrong."
Roland replies   with laughter loud and long. AOI

XXII

Count Ganelon,   when he hears Roland laugh,
Suffers such pain   he nearly splits with rage,

277. Ganelon is indeed Roland's stepfather, but the word used here, *parrastre*, is an insulting one; similarly, *fillastre* in line 743.

And he comes close   to falling in a faint.
He says to Roland,   "Now count me not your friend,
For you have swayed   this council to your will!
My rightful king,   you see me here at hand,
Ready to do   whatever you command.   AOI

XXIII

"To Saragossa   I know that I must go.   *310*
And from that journey   no man comes to his home.
Remember this: your sister is my wife;
She bore my son—   there is no fairer youth—
His name is Baldwin;   he'll make a valiant man.
To him I leave   my fiefdoms, all my lands.
Grant him your care;   I'll see him not again."
Then answers Charles,   "You have too soft a heart.
You know my will;   it's time for you to start."   AOI

XXIV

Thus spoke the king,   "Come forward, Ganelon.
Take now from me   the envoy's staff and glove: *320*
You've heard the Franks,   and they have chosen you."
Says Ganelon,   "Sire, this is Roland's work;
I'll have no love,   as long as I may live,
Either for him   or Oliver his friend.
All the twelve peers,   to whom he is so dear,
Sire, in your presence,   I challenge here and now!"
Then says the king,   "You yield too much to wrath.
Now you shall go,   since that is my command."
"I'll have the same   protection from Marsile
You gave Basant   and his brother Basile."   AOI   *330*

---

317. Charles's irritated reply seems astonishing; one wonders if it does
not conceal his embarrassed unwillingness to admit, once Ganelon has,
to Charles's relief, been chosen, that the mission is indeed extremely
dangerous.

XXV

The Emperor Charles   holds out his right-hand glove,
But Ganelon,   who'd rather not be there,
Taking the gauntlet,   lets it fall to the ground.
The Frenchmen say,   "Oh, God! What does this mean?
Surely this message   will bring us to our woe."
Says Ganelon,   "Your answer won't be slow."

XXVI

"Sire," says the count,   "now grant me leave to go;
Since go I must,   I care not for delay."
The king replies,   "In Jesu's name and mine!"
340   Then Charles' right hand   absolves the count from sin;
The staff and letter   are both given to him.

XXVII

Count Ganelon   returning to his tent,
Arrays himself   as if for waging war
With the best arms   his household can provide.
The spurs are gold   he fastens to his feet,
Murglais, his sword,   is hanging at his side,
And now he mounts   his war-horse Tachebrun,
The stirrup held   by his uncle Guinemer.
Then you could see   how many knights shed tears,
350   All of them saying,   "Alas! You go to die.
Long have you served   the great king at his court,
A noble vassal;   none fail to speak your praise.
The man who named you   the envoy to Marsile
Will not live long—   in spite of Charlemagne!
Roland was wrong   not to remember this:
Behind you stands   a mighty family."

340. One of several examples in the poem of Charlemagne's **priestly**
function.

And then they say, "Let us go with you, lord."
The count replies, "Almighty God forbid!
I'll die alone,   not sacrifice good knights.
But you must go,   my lords, back to sweet France   360
Where you will bring   my greetings to my wife,
To Pinabel,   my good friend and my peer,
And to my son,   Baldwin, whom you all know—
Give him your help,   and serve him as your lord."
Now toward Marsile   Ganelon sets his course. AOI

XXVIII

Ganelon rides   under tall olive trees;
Now he has met   the envoys from Marsile,
And Blancandrin   is riding at his side;
Both of them talk   with great diplomacy.
Says Blancandrin,   "I marvel at your king—   370
For he has conquered   the whole of Italy,
And then to England   he crossed the salty sea
So that the Saxons   would pay Saint Peter's fee.
And what of Spain   will Charlemagne require?"
The count replies,   "That's hidden in his mind.
A greater king   no man will ever find." AOI

XXIX

Says Blancandrin,   "The Franks are noble men;
But they do wrong,   those warlike dukes and counts
When by the counsel   they give to Charlemagne
They wear him out,   and others suffer too."   380

359. Ganelon's nobility here may possibly be motivated by the "little trick" he is plotting. Otherwise it is an example, among many in the text, of the poet's insistance on adversaries of equal weight.
375. At his trial, Ganelon will insist that he was always loyal to Charlemagne. His conversations with Blancandrin and Marsile show him punctiliously respectful to the Emperor, and often convincingly admiring: the most splendid praise of Charles in the poem comes from Ganelon (*laisse* XL).

Ganelon says, "Of this I could accuse
Only Count Roland— who'll pay for it some day.
Not long ago, when Charles sat at his ease,
His nephew came dressed in his battle gear—
He'd gone for plunder somewhere near Carcasonne.
In Roland's hand an apple shone, bright red;
He told his uncle, 'Accept it, my fair lord!
I bring you here the crowns of every king.'
But his great pride will lead him on too far,
390   For every day we see him risk his life.
If he were killed, there'd be an end to strife." AOI

XXX

Says Blancandrin, "Evil is Roland's heart.
He'd have the world surrender to his will,
Proclaim his right to every land on earth!
But by whose help can he attempt so much?"
"The Franks of France! He so commands their love,
They'll never fail him, they're with him to a man.
He gives them gifts of silver and much gold,
War-horses, mules, brocades and costly arms;
400   The king himself won't cross him in the least:
By Roland's sword he'll rule to the far East!" AOI

XXXI

So Ganelon and Blancandrin ride on
Until they've made a solemn pact: they vow
That they will seek to have Count Roland slain.
They go their way, and then dismount at last
In Saragossa where a tall yew tree stands.
Under a pine a throne has been set up,
Draped in brocade of Alexandrian silk.
There sits the king, the ruler of all Spain;

400. This line could also mean that Roland gives the Emperor everything the latter wants, which is equally true.

Around him wait   his twenty thousand men.   *410*
Not one of them   lets fall a single word;
They're all intent   on what they hope to hear
From those two men   who even now appear.

XXXII

Now Blancandrin   has come before Marsile,
And by the fist   he holds Count Ganelon.
He speaks these words: "Hail, in Mohammed's name,
Apollo's too,   whose Law we all obey!
We have delivered   your message to King Charles;
When he had heard us,   he raised his hands on high
To praise his God,   but gave us no reply.   *420*
Now he has sent you   one of his noble lords,
A count of France,   a man of power and wealth.
From him you'll learn   if there is hope for peace."
Marsile replies,   "We'll hear him; let him speak."

XXXIII

Count Ganelon   has taken careful thought,
Now he begins   in well-considered words,
Subtly contrived—   the count knows how to talk.
He tells Marsile: "May God grant you His grace,
That glorious Lord   to whom all men must pray!
Now by the will   of Charlemagne the King,   *430*
You must accept   the holy Christian law,
And half of Spain   he'll let you hold in fief.
Should you refuse   agreement to these terms,
You'll find yourself   a captive and in chains,

425 ff. Ganelon is not only an accomplished liar but an enthusiastic
one (see his description of the death of the Caliph, in *laisse* LIV). Here
only the tone would seem to misrepresent Charlemagne, except that
Marsile will be allowed to keep only half of Spain, in fief to Charles;
the other half is to be ruled by Roland. Thus the latter is made, once
again, the focal point of the pagans' anger.

Taken by force   to answer Charles at Aix.
There you'll be judged,   and you will be condemned
To die a death   of infamy and shame."
At that Marsile   in fear and fury raised
A throwing spear—   its feathering was gold;
440 He would have struck,   but that his men took hold. AOI

XXXIV

In the king's face   they see the color change;
He stands there raging,   shaking his javelin.
Ganelon's hand   reaches to grasp his sword,
Out of the scabbard   draws it two finger lengths;
He tells the blade: "Shining you are, and fair!
Long have we served,   we two, at King Charles' court!
The Emperor of France   shall never say
I died alone   here in this foreign land
Before their best   have bought you at your price."
450 The pagans say,   "We must not let them fight!"

XXXV

The Saracens   prevail upon Marsile
Until the king   will take his seat again.
Said the caliph,   "You don't do any good
When you are ready   to strike the Frenchman down.
Just let him speak,   and listen to him well."
Ganelon says,   "My lord, I'll suffer that.
But I won't stop,   for all the gold God made,
For all the treasure   that's gathered in this land,
Before I give him,   if he will grant me time,
460 The message Charles   confided to my care,
The words he sends   his mortal enemy."
Ganelon wore   a cloak of sable furs
Covered in folds   of Alexandrian silk.
He throws it down—   it's caught by Blancandrin—
But has no thought   of letting go his sword:

His right hand grasps   the handle made of gold.
The pagans say,   "Noble he is, and bold!" AOI

XXXVI

Count Ganelon   stands close beside the king,
And says to him,   "You have no cause for wrath
If Charlemagne   who rules the land of France   470
Says you must take   the holy Christian law:
One half of Spain   he'll let you hold in fief,
His nephew Roland   will rule the other part—
There you will have   a partner full of pride!
If you refuse   agreement to these terms,
In Saragossa   you soon will be besieged,
You'll find yourself   a prisoner in chains,
And straight away   you'll be led off to Aix.
And then no palfrey,   no war-horse will you have,
Nor yet a mule   to ride with dignity,   480
But you'll be thrown   onto some pack-beast's back,
And lose your head   at that long journey's end.
Here is the message   I've brought at Charles' command."
He puts the letter   into Marsile's right hand.

XXXVII

Now King Marsile,   his face gone white with rage,
Breaks the seal open   and throws the wax away,
Looks at the letter   and sees what it contains.
"Thus writes King Charles   who rules the land of France:
He won't forget   his anger and his grief
About Basant   and his brother Basile   490
Whose heads I took   on a hill near Haltilie.
If I would make amends,   there's just one way:

485. Jenkins' reading here is *escolez de lire*, "had been taught how to
read." The fact is in any case verified by line 487. The letter itself, if
Marsile gives us its full contents, asks only for the one proof of sub-
mission, which Marsile does not provide.

I'll have to send him   my uncle, the Caliph;
If I refuse,   he'll have no love for me."
His son spoke up   and said to King Marsile,
"Wild empty words   we've had from Ganelon,
He's gone too far—   he well deserves to die.
Leave him to me,   and I'll do what is right."
Then Ganelon   prepared for the attack,
500   Brandished his sword,   the pine tree at his back.

XXXVIII

Into an orchard   the pagan king retired,
And with him went   the wisest of his men.
Blancandrin came   whose heavy beard was grey,
And Jurfaret,   Marsile's own son and heir,
And the Caliph,   his uncle and good friend.
Says Blancandrin,   "Summon the Frenchman here—
I have his word   that he will serve our cause."
Marsile replies,   "Then bring him to me now."
Blancandrin takes   the count by the right hand,
510   Walks through the orchard,   and leads him to Marsile.
They plot the treason   that cunning will conceal.   AOI

XXXIX

Thus speaks the king: "My fair lord Ganelon,
I know I did   an ill-considered thing
When in my rage   I went to strike you down.
I pledge you now   by these fine sable furs—
The gold they're trimmed with   is worth five hundred pounds:
Tomorrow evening   I'll have made fair amends."
Says Ganelon,   "Your gift I won't refuse.
And if God please,   by this you shall not lose!"   AOI

XL

520   Then says Marsile,   "Know that I speak the truth,
Count Ganelon;   I want to be your friend.

Now will you tell me   something of Charlemagne.
Old as he is,   his time must have run out—
I know he's lived   more than two hundred years.
He has made journeys   to so many far lands,
So many blows   he's taken on his shield,
He has made beggars   of so many rich kings—
When will he ever   give up and take his rest?"
The count replies,   "He's not as you suppose.
No one who sees him   and learns to know him well   530
Can fail to say   the emperor is great.
My words won't give you   the measure of this man—
His noble virtues   are far beyond my praise—
And who could put   his courage into speech!
By God's grace honor   illuminates my lord:
He'd rather die   than break faith with his court.

XLI

The pagan says,   "Truly, I am amazed
By Charlemagne   whose hair is grey with age—
I know he's lived   more than two hundred years.
He's dragged his body   through so many far lands,   540
Taken such blows   from lances and from spears,
So many kings   reduced to beggary,
It must be time   for him to look for peace."
"That will not happen   while Roland is alive;
There's no such vassal   under the high-domed sky;
And very brave   is Oliver his friend.
While the twelve peers   whom Charlemagne so loves

544. Here again Ganelon insists that only Roland is responsible for
the pagans' misfortunes, and prepares the accomplishment of his own
revenge, which depends on the separation of Roland and Charles.
While the motive for this may be practical, as Marsile obviously could
not hope to defeat the Emperor's entire army even with Ganelon's
help, it seems that Ganelon really has no grudge against Charles in
spite of the latter's obvious lack of enthusiasm for him. It should be
remembered that Ganelon's wife is Charles's sister, and Roland's mother.

Serve as his vanguard   with twenty thousand knights,
The king is safe;   he fears no man alive."   AOI

XLII

550 The pagan says,   "Now marvelous indeed
Is Charlemagne   whose hair has grown so white—
He is at least   two hundred years of age.
When he has conquered   so many distant lands,
Has taken blows   from so many sharp spears,
And such great kings   brought to defeat and death,
Is he not ready   to take his rest at home?"
The count replies,   "Not while his nephew lives.
There's none so valiant   from here to the far East.
A great lord too   is Oliver his friend.
560 While the twelve peers,   for whom Charles feels such love,
Serve him and lead   those twenty thousand Franks,
Charles can be sure   no foe will break his ranks."

XLIII

"Fair Ganelon,"   then says the pagan king,
"You'll see no soldiers   better at war than mine,
And I can summon   four hundred thousand knights.
Can I not fight   King Charles and all his Franks?"
"If you should try it,"   Count Ganelon replies,
"I tell you this,   you'd massacre your men.
Forget that folly,   and hear what I advise:
570 To Charlemagne   send such a royal gift
As to amaze   and gratify the French.
Send twenty men   as hostages for you,
And then the king   will go home to sweet France.
Behind his army   the rear-guard will remain,
And with them Roland,   the nephew of the king,
And Oliver,   so gallant and so brave.
And there they die—   if you'll do as I say.
King Charles will see   the downfall of his pride;
He'll have no wish   to carry on the fight."   AOI

XLIV

Answers Marsile,   "My fair lord Ganelon,   *580*
Tell me the way   Count Roland can be killed."
Ganelon says,   "Here is the plan I've made:
The king will cross   the mountain pass at Cize,
With a strong guard   remaining far behind.
He'll leave his nephew,   Count Roland, in the rear,
Oliver too,   in whom he has such faith,
With them a host   of twenty thousand Franks.
Then of your pagans,   a hundred thousand men
Must be sent out   to launch the first attack.
You'll see the Frenchmen   wounded and overcome—   *590*
Not that I say   your men won't suffer too.
If you attack   a second time that way,
You can be sure   that Roland won't escape.
Once you have done   this brave and knightly deed,
All your life long   from warfare you'll be freed."

XLV

"With that same blow   that struck Count Roland down,
You would cut off   the Emperor's right arm;
His mighty host   you'd scatter and destroy,
Nor would he find   so great a force again.
All of his Empire   would be restored to peace."   *600*
Marsile fell on his neck;   with joy he swore
That Ganelon   should loot his treasure-store.   AOI

---

580. Jenkins supplies *ço dist li reis Marsílies* from V⁴, as the line is
incomplete in the Oxford manuscript. V⁴ is an assonanced version of
the *Roland* in 6012 lines. Jenkins uses it to correct certain defects in
the Oxford manuscript when a corresponding line can be located.
600. Following Jenkins I have translated *Tere Maior* as "the Empire"
throughout. Bédier calls it *la terre des Aieux*, "land of our fathers."
602. Bédier does not translate this line (*Puis si cumencet a venir ses
tresors*). It seems clear enough, however, that Marsile is about to
offer material expression of his delight.

XLVI

Then says Marsile,   "There's one thing more to do,
Since all good counsel   depends on perfect trust;
Give me your oath   that Roland is to die."
Ganelon says,   "That shall be as you wish."
He swore by relics   he carried in his sword,
And so forever   turned from his rightful lord.   AOI

XLVII

   A throne was there,   made all of ivory.
610 A book was brought   by King Marsile's command:
Laws of Mohammed   and Tervagant, his gods.
On this he swore,   the Spanish Saracen,
If he found Roland   was named to the rear-guard,
He would attack   with all his pagan knights,
And do his utmost   to see the Frenchman die.
"Amen to that!"   was Ganelon's reply.

XLVIII

There was a pagan,   his name was Valdabron,
Who now approached,   and stood before Marsile.
Laughing for joy,   he said to Ganelon:
620 "Here is my sword,   a better you'll not find;
The hilt is worth   a thousand coins of gold!
I give you this   for friendship's sake, fair lord;

603-4. Bédier's translation expresses the same meaning, but words missing from the two lines are supplied by Jenkins.

611. The spelling of this and many other proper names varies throughout the text. Bédier reproduces all the variants, but I have preferred to adopt the most frequently used versions.

621. The line in the Oxford manuscript seems to mean that counting its two parts (*entre les helz*), the hilt is worth a thousand *mangons*. Bédier, however, considers this an abbreviation of the fact, mentioned in 1570, that Valdabron gave Ganelon a sword *and* a thousand *mangons*.

If you will help us,   we cannot fail to find
The valiant Roland   commanding the rear-guard."
The count replies,   "You'll find him there, and win."
Then they exchange   kisses on cheek and chin.

XLIX

Afterward came   a man called Climorin.
Laughing for joy,   he said to Ganelon:
"Now take my helmet—   none better have I seen—
For with your help   in showing us the way,   630
We'll bring great Roland   to his defeat and shame."
Ganelon said,   "You won't have far to seek."
Then they exchanged   kisses on lips and cheek.   AOI

L

Then came the queen,   the lady Bramimonde.
"My lord," she said,   "I count myself your friend,
The king admires you,   and so do all his men.
Give to your wife   these necklaces from me,
Heavy with gold,   jacinths and amethysts—
A greater prize   than all the wealth of Rome,
And none so fine   has Charles who rules the Franks."   640
He put them in his boots,   and gave her thanks.   AOI

LI

Then the king summons   his treasurer Malduit:
"Have they prepared   the tribute for King Charles?"
"The seven hundred camels,   by your command,
Have all been loaded   with silver and with gold,
And twenty men,   our noblest, set to go."   AOI

641. It would indeed seem uncomfortable, as Sayers points out, to
carry heavy jewelry in one's boots, but this translation of *hoese* is
accepted by most editors. Jenkins mentions that Duke Naimon in
Aspremont carries a griffon's paw in his "hose," so discomfort must
have been irrelevant.

LII

King Marsile places   his arm around the count,
Saying to him,   "Valiant you are, and wise.
But as you keep   your God's most holy law,
650   I charge you never   to turn your heart from me!
Of all I own   I'll give you a good part:
Ten mules are loaded   with fine Arabian gold,
And every year   you'll have as much again.
Give Charles the keys   to this broad city's walls,
Tell him its treasures   will henceforth be his own,
And then name Roland   commander of the guard.
If I can find him   crossing some narrow pass,
There I'll attack   and fight him to the death."
Ganelon says,   "Then let us speed the day."
660   He mounts his horse,   and quickly rides away.   AOI

LIII

The Emperor Charles   has now retraced his steps
As far as Galne—   that was a captured town
Whose walls Count Roland   had leveled to the ground;
No one would live there   for the next hundred years.
He waits for news   of Ganelon's return,
And for the tribute   offered to him by Spain.
At dawn one morning,   just as the sky grows light,
Count Ganelon   comes back from his long ride.   AOI

LIV

The Emperor Charles   rose early on that day.
670   Now, having prayed   at matins and a mass,
He goes outside   and stands on the green grass.
Roland is with him,   the noble Oliver,
Naimon the Duke,   and many others too.

Ganelon comes,   treacherous and forsworn.
All of his cunning   he puts into his speech,
Saying to Charles,   "I greet you in God's name!
Here are the keys   to King Marsile's fair town;
From Saragossa,   treasures beyond all price,
And twenty nobles,   hostages—guard them well!
But King Marsile   has asked me to explain   680
Why you won't see   his uncle, the Caliph:
Before my eyes   a hundred thousand men
All armed in mail,   some with their helmets closed,
Swords at their belts,   the hilts inlaid with gold,
Sailed with that lord   out to the open sea.
They fled Marsile,   hating the Christian law
Which they refused   to honor and to keep.
They sailed away,   but had not gone four leagues
When they were caught   in such a frightful storm
They all were drowned.   So perished the Caliph.   690
Were he alive,   he'd be here with me now.
As for Marsile,   my lord, you can be sure
That well before   a single month has passed,
He'll follow you   when you return to France.
There he'll accept   the Faith that you uphold,
Both of his hands   he'll place between your own,
And do you homage   for all his lands in Spain."
Then said the king,   "For this may God be thanked!
You have done well,   and great shall be your prize."
Among the hosts,   a thousand trumpets sound;   700
The French break camp,   they load each mule and horse,
And toward sweet France   they gladly set their course. AOI

680 ff. This account of the Caliph's death is obviously a fiction created
to explain his failure to accompany Ganelon. According to Jenkins, the
copyist of the Oxford manuscript made the mistake of believing Ganelon,
and for that reason replaced "the Caliph" with "Marganice" when he
appears at Roncevaux (1915).

LV

King Charles the Great   has conquered all of Spain,
Captured its forts,   its cities laid to waste;
His war, he says,   has now come to its end.
The emperor rides   once more toward his sweet France.
From Roland's spearhead   the flag of battle flies;
When, from a hilltop,   it waves against the sky,
The French make camp   throughout the countryside.
710 Pagans are riding   through valleys deep and dark,
Their coats of mail   are laced up to the chin,
Their helmets closed;   bright swords hang at their sides,
Shields at their necks,   a pennon on each lance;
Where trees grow thick   high on a hill they wait,
Four hundred thousand   watching for day's first light.
Alas! If only   the French could see that sight!   AOI

LVI

The day is over,   the night grows calm and still.
The Emperor Charles   goes to his bed and sleeps.
In dream he rides   through the great pass at Cize;
720 Clasped in his hands   he holds an ashwood spear:
Count Ganelon   wrenches it from his grasp,
With raging strength   shatters and breaks the wood,
And sends the splinters   flying against the sky.
King Charles sleeps on,   not opening his eyes.

LVII

After that dream   another vision came:
He was in France,   in his chapel at Aix.
A vicious beast   was biting his right arm.
Out of the forest   he sees a leopard run,
And he himself   it cruelly attacks.

703. The poet returns to the beginning of his story, as also in line
2610.

From his great hall   a boarhound rushes out   730
And comes to Charles,   running with leaps and bounds,
Seizes the beast,   biting off its right ear,
And in its fury   attacks the leopard too.
The Frenchmen watch   the mighty battle rage,
But they don't know   which side will win the fight.
King Charles sleeps on,   and does not wake all night. AOI

LVIII

Darkness of night   gives way to shining dawn.
Throughout the host,   clarion trumpets sound.
Proud, on his horse,   the emperor appears.
"Barons, my lords,"   says Charlemagne the King,   740
"Narrow and dark   will be this mountain pass—
Who shall remain   to guard us from the rear?"
Ganelon says,   "Choose Roland, my stepson.
You have no baron   as valorous as he."
Fiercely the king   looks at the one who spoke,
And says to him: "Vile demon that you are!
You are insane,   possessed by deadly rage!
And in the vanguard—   who'll have the leader's place?"
Ganelon says,   "Count Ogier the Dane.
None would do better,   and no one can complain."   750

LIX

Count Roland heard   what Ganelon proposed,
And then he answered   with knightly courtesy:
"Noble stepfather,   now I must hold you dear,
For you have named me   commander of this guard.
The King of France   won't lose by my neglect
War-horse or palfrey,   that I can promise you;

---

738. Jenkins supplies the end of this line, *sonent menut cil graisle* from
V⁴V⁷, since the Oxford reading is unintelligible.
750. "And no one can complain" is implied in the text, although it
is not stated.

He shall not lose   a single riding-mule,
Saddle-horse, pack-horse—   none shall give up its life
Until our swords   take payment for that prize."
760   Ganelon says,   "I know you tell no lies."   AOI

LX

When Roland heard   he'd stay with the rear-guard,
To his stepfather   he angrily replied:
"Ignoble serf,   despicable foul wretch,
Do you suppose   I'll let the glove fall here
The way you dropped the staff   at King Charles' feet?"   AOI

LXI

"My rightful lord,"   says Roland to the king,
"Give me the bow   you're holding in your hand;
I promise you   that no man here will say
I let it fall,   like Ganelon that day
770   The envoy's staff   dropped out of his right hand."
The Emperor Charles   sits with his head bowed low,

---

761. *Laisse* LX occurs only in the Oxford manuscript, and seems an
unlikely contradiction of Roland's usual gallantry (of which he has
just given an example). Jenkins believes the *laisse* to be unauthentic,
and points out that Ganelon had let fall a glove and not a staff. This
same mistake is reproduced, however, in the following *laisse*. Bédier
attributes the vigor of Roland's reply to his concern lest Ganelon not
understand the irony of the preceding *laisse*. The poet would have
used this means to emphasize the fact that Roland was never in any
doubt about Ganelon's intentions. It seems to me sufficiently apparent,
without this, that no one could have been. Only the fact that Ganelon
had previously accepted Roland's nomination makes it impossible for
Charles to act on his immediate suspicions. He would also have
hesitated to believe that Ganelon, violent as he was, would dare to
betray Roland while he himself remained with Charles.
767. The bow is a symbol of command.

Pulls his moustache,   and strokes his long white beard,
While in his eyes   unwilling tears appear.

LXII

At that Duke Naimon   stood up to speak his mind—
The court could boast   no better man than he—
Saying to Charles,   "You have heard what's been said;
It's clear enough   that Roland is enraged.
He has been named   to go with the rear-guard;
You have no baron   who will dispute that now.
Give him the bow   that you yourself have bent;   780
Then choose good men   to fight at his command."
Charles puts the bow   in Roland's outstretched hand.

LXIII

The Emperor Charles   calls Roland to come forth.
"My noble nephew,   this is what I intend:
Half of my army   shall stay behind with you.
Accept their service,   and then you will be safe."
Count Roland answers,   "Never will I agree.
May God destroy me,   if I so shame my race!
Just twenty thousand   shall serve me, valiant Franks.
You'll cross the mountains,   safely in France arrive—   790
And fear no man   as long as I'm alive!" AOI

LXIV

Roland has mounted   the horse he rides to war.
There comes to join him   his friend Count Oliver,
And Gerin comes,   the brave Count Gerier,
And Oton comes,   with him Count Bérengier,
And Astor comes,   and fiery Anseïs,
And old Gérard,   the Count of Roussillon,

773. Although Charlemagne tries to restrain his tears, they obviously
do him credit: sensitivity was no sign of weakness in a warrior.
Roland, in *laisse* CXL, weeps for the dead Franks "like a noble knight."
774. Duke Naimon's advice is always followed, usually to disaster.

The powerful and wealthy   Duke Gaïfier.
Says the Archbishop,   "My head on it, I'll go!"
800   "And I am with you,"   answers Count Gautier,
"I'm Roland's vassal—   my help is his by right."
Then they select   the twenty thousand knights.   AOI

LXV

Count Roland says   to Gautier de l'Hum:
"A thousand Franks,   men of our land, you'll take
To occupy   the hills and the ravines,
So that King Charles   may safely go his way."   AOI
Gautier answers,   "For you I'll do my best."
Leading away   a thousand Franks of France,
Gautier will guard   the mountains and ravines;
810   Whatever happens,   he won't come down again
Without a battle—   Almaris of Belferne
Gave them a fight;   and seven hundred blades
Flashed from their scabbards   on that most evil day.

LXVI

High are the hills,   deep valleys shun the light;
The cliffs rise grey,   the gorges hold dark fear.
The French ride on   in misery and pain,
Their passing heard   some fifteen leagues around;
And when once more   they're back again in France,
In Gascony,   where Charlemagne is lord,
820   Then they remember   the lands they hold, their sons,
Their maiden daughters,   their fair and noble wives—
There is not one   who is not moved to weep
But of them all   none sorrows as does Charles,
For he has left   his nephew there in Spain;
And now his tears   the king cannot restrain.   AOI

LXVII

All the twelve peers   have stayed behind in Spain;
They guard the pass   with twenty thousand Franks,

Courageous men   who do not fear to die.
And now King Charles   is riding home again;
He drapes his cloak   to hide his grieving face.   830
Duke Naimon rides   next to the emperor;
He says to Charles,   "What weighs your spirits down?"
The king replies,   "Who asks me that does wrong.
I can't keep silent   the sorrow that I feel,
For Ganelon   will be the doom of France.
Last night an angel   sent me a warning dream:
I held a spear—   he broke it from my grasp,
That count who named   my nephew to the guard.
And I left Roland   among that pagan race—
God! If I lose him,   no one can take his place."   AOI   840

LXVIII

Charlemagne weeps;   he can't hold back his tears.
They grieve for him,   his hundred thousand Franks,
And for Count Roland   are suddenly afraid.
A traitor's lies   left him to die in Spain—
Rich gifts the pagan   bestowed on Ganelon:
Silver and gold,   brocades and silken cloaks,
Camels and lions,   fine horses, riding mules.
Now King Marsile   summons the lords of Spain,
His counts and viscounts,   his chieftains and his dukes,
His high emirs,   and all their warrior sons: 850
Four hundred thousand   assemble in three days.
In Saragossa   the drums begin to sound;
They place Mohammed   high on the citadel—
No pagan fails   to worship him and pray.
And then they ride   with all their might and main
Through Terre Certaine,   through valleys, over hills,
Until they see   the battle-flags of France.

---

848. This admirable transition should be noted: from the unproven
but accurate presentiments of the Franks to the actual preparations
of Marsile.

The twelve companions are waiting with the guard;
When they are challenged, the fighting will be hard.

LXIX

860 King Marsile's nephew rides up before the host.
Laughing, he prods his mule with a sharp goad,
And to his uncle addresses this fair speech:
"For years, Lord King, I've served you faithfully;
My only wages were hardships, suffering,
And battles fought and won on many fields.
I ask this boon: have Roland left to me!
I'll take his life on my sharp-pointed spear,
And if Mohammed protects me in the fight,
The land of Spain once more shall be our own,
870 From the high passes as far as Durestant!
Charles will be weary, the Frenchmen will retreat;
In all your lifetime, war will not touch your land."
King Marsile places the gauntlet in his hand. AOI

LXX

King Marsile's nephew, the gauntlet in his fist,
Speaks to his uncle in proud and fiery words:
"You've given me, fair Sire, a noble gift.
Choose for me now the twelve among your lords
Who'll meet in battle with the twelve peers of France."
First of them all, Duke Falsaron replies—
880 This Saracen was brother to Marsile—
He says, "Fair nephew, both you and I will go,
And they'll find out what fighting really means.
The rear-guard waits, protecting Charlemagne;
When we attack, those Franks will all be slain!" AOI

866. Marsile's nephew, whose name we learn later is Aelroth, asks for first blow against Roland.
877. Including himself, as the twelve French peers include Roland.

LXXI

King Corsalis   comes forward in his turn.
He is a Berber,   and skilled in the black arts.
He speaks up now,   a vassal true and brave—
For all God's gold   he'd never run away.
Spurring, there comes   Malprimis de Brigant,
Faster on foot   than any horse can run.   *890*
Before Marsile   he stands and shouts aloud:
"At Roncevaux   my war-cry shall resound—
If I find Roland,   I'll leave him on the ground!"   AOI

LXXII

Comes an emir,   the lord of Balaguer,
A handsome man,   his face serene and bold.
Whoever sees him   riding his horse to war,
Bearing his arms   with courage and great pride,
Knows that this hero   well deserves his fame;
If he were Christian,   he'd be a noble knight.
Before Marsile   he stops and cries aloud,   *900*
"I'll take myself   to Roncevaux and fight!
If I find Roland,   there he shall lose his life,
Oliver too,   and all of the twelve peers.
The French will die   in sorrow and great shame.
Now Charlemagne grows old,   weak in his mind;
He'll have no wish   to carry on the war—
In all of Spain   we'll see no more of Franks."
For that fair speech,   Marsile gave many thanks.   AOI

LXXIII

Then an emir   who came from Moriane—

888. It would seem that the Oxford manuscript omits here the actual
words of Corsalis, who, like the other Saracen lords, makes a boasting
speech in other manuscripts.

910   There was no man   more evil in all Spain—
Rode to Marsile   and made his boasting speech:
"To Roncevaux   I'll lead my company,
All twenty thousand   with lances and stout shields;
If I find Roland,   his death is a sure thing,
And every day   that loss will grieve his king."   AOI

LXXIV

And then rides forth   Torgis of Tortelose,
He is a count,   the ruler of that town;
His heart desires   to work the Christian's doom,
And with the others   he stands before Marsile,
920   Telling the king: "We'll triumph—have no fear!
Against Mohammed   Saint Peter has no chance:
Give him your prayers,   and we will take the field.
At Roncevaux   Roland shall meet my steel,
And then no man   can save him from quick death.
Look at my sword—   how keen it is, and long;
When this blade strikes   against proud Durendal,
You'll soon be hearing   which one of them went down!
The Franks will die   who meet our men in war,
Leaving old Charles,   whom shame and grief confound,
930   To live his days   a king without a crown."

LXXV

And then rides forth   Escrimiz of Valterne,
That is the fief   held by this Saracen.
His voice rings out   above the crowd of men:
"At Roncevaux   I'll bring the French pride down!
If I find Roland,   he won't leave with his head,
Nor Oliver,   who leads so many men.
All the twelve peers   now stand condemned to die;
The French are lost—   all France will feel their lack—
Charles will be needing   good vassals at his back."   AOI

LXXVI

And then rides forth   the pagan Estorgant—   *940*
His sworn companion   Estramariz comes too—
Fell traitors both,   famed for their lying tongues.
Then says the king,   "Come forward, my good lords!
Over the mountains   you'll ride to Roncevaux,
Taking your place   as leaders of my men."
And they reply,   "My lord, at your command!
We will attack   Roland and Oliver;
Nothing can save   the twelve peers from swift death.
Here are our swords,   keen are their blades and strong;
Soon we will stain them   bright crimson with hot blood!   *950*
The French will die,   and Charlemagne know grief,
All of his Empire   we'll give you for your own.
Come with us, Sire,   and witness their defeat—
We'll have King Charles,   a captive, at your feet."

LXXVII

And then comes running   Margariz of Seville—
He has the land   as far as Cazmarines—
A man so handsome   no lady can resist:
None, in his presence,   but feels inclined toward love,
Or when she sees him   refuses him a smile.
He is the best   of all the pagan knights.   *960*
His voice rings out   above the swelling crowd
To tell the king,   "Now have no fear, my lord!
At Roncevaux   Count Roland will be slain

955. The most charming of the pagans—perhaps of all the knights—
Margariz alone does not die on the battlefield, but vanishes, at least
from the Oxford manuscript, after attacking Oliver (1318). Evidence
from other versions suggested to Bédier that Margariz was spared to
be the messenger who would tell Marsile the fate of his first army,
but the location of this probable lacuna in the Oxford manuscript could
not be determined.

By my own hand,   as Oliver shall die;
The twelve peers all   shall have their martyrdom.
Look at my sword—   its hilt is made of gold—
A noble gift   from the Emir of Primes;
I swear to you   I'll sheathe it in red blood.
The Franks will die,   and France be brought to shame.
970   Old Charlemagne   whose flowing beard is white
Shall live his days   in sorrow and in wrath.
Within a year   we'll conquer all of France—
We'll go to bed   in Saint Denis' own town."
The pagan king,   in gratitude, bows down. AOI

LXXVIII

And then comes forward   Chernuble de Munigre;
His hair's so long   it sweeps the very ground.
Sometimes, for fun,   he'll carry on his back
Burdens enough   to overload four mules.
In that far country   from which he comes, they say
980   The sun won't shine,   no wheat will ever grow,
Rain never falls,   nor is there any dew;
The rocks and stones   in all the land are black:
Some, for that reason,   call it the devil's home.
Chernuble says,   "My sword is at my side;
At Roncevaux   I'll stain its keen blade red.
If I should find   great Roland on my way,
I'll challenge him—   or trust me not again—
And my sharp blade   will conquer Durendal.
The Franks will die,   and France see them no more."
990   And at these words   the twelve peers take command.
They lead away   a hundred thousand men,
All of them eager   to form the battle lines.
They put on armor,   inside a grove of pines.

LXXIX

The pagans wear   Saracen coats of mail,
Most of them furnished   with triple-layered chains.

From Saragossa   come the good helms they lace;
They gird on swords   whose steel comes from Vienne;
Their shields are strong;   Valencia made their spears;
Their battle flags   are crimson, blue and white.
All mules and palfreys   must now be left behind;   1000
Each mounts his war-horse;   in close-knit ranks they ride.
Fair is the day,   the sun shines bright and clear,
Weapons and armor   glitter with fiery light,
A thousand trumpets   command more splendor still.
That great shrill clamor   reaches the Frenchmen's camp.
Oliver says,   "Companion, it would seem
That we will have   some Saracens to fight."
Roland replies,   "God grant that you be right!
Here we will stand,   defending our great king.
This is the service   a vassal owes his lord: 1010
To suffer hardships,   endure great heat and cold,
And in a battle   to lose both hair and hide.
Now every Frank   prepare to strike great blows—
Let's hear no songs   that mock us to our shame!
Pagans are wrong,   the Christian cause is right.
A bad example   I'll be in no man's sight."   AOI

LXXX

Count Oliver   has climbed up on a hill.
From there he searches   the valley to his right,
And sees that host   of pagan Saracens.
Then he calls out   to Roland, his sworn friend: 1020
"Coming from Spain   I see the fiery glow
Of shining hauberks,   the blazing steel of helms.
For our brave Franks   this means great toil and pain.

1016. Roland says he will not serve as an exemplum, that is, a cautionary
tale, in the wrong sense.
1021. "Glow" follows Jenkins' *brunor*; Bédier has *bruur*, which he
translates *rumeur*.
1022. *Blanc* often has the sense of "bright" or "shining," rather than
"white."

And that foul traitor,   false-hearted Ganelon,
Knew this—that's why   he named us to the guard."
Count Roland answers,   "Stop, Oliver, be still!
Of my stepfather   I'll let no man speak ill."

LXXXI

Count Oliver   has climbed up on a hill;
From there he sees   the Spanish lands below,
1030   And Saracens   assembled in great force.
Their helmets gleam   with gold and precious stones,
Their shields are shining,   their hauberks burnished gold,
Their long sharp spears   with battle flags unfurled.
He tries to see   how many men there are:
Even battalions   are more than he can count.
And in his heart   Oliver is dismayed;
Quick as he can,   he comes down from the height,
And tells the Franks   what they will have to fight.

LXXXII

Oliver says,   "Here come the Saracens—
1040   A greater number   no man has ever seen!
The first host carries   a hundred thousand shields.
Their helms are laced,   their hauberks shining white,
From straight wood handles   rise ranks of burnished spears.
You'll have a battle   like none on earth before!
Frenchmen, my lords,   now God give you the strength
To stand your ground,   and keep us from defeat."
They say, "God's curse   on those who quit the field!
We're yours till death—   not one of us will yield."   AOI

1031. That is, jewels set in gold—the invariable phrase.
1032. Safré: Here again Bédier and Jenkins disagree about yellow and
blue, the latter interpreting safré to mean bordered with blue (the word
being related to "sapphire"), while Bédier's interpretation, the more
generally accepted, has it a yellow or golden dye.

LXXXIII

Oliver says, "The pagan might is great—
It seems to me, our Franks are very few!   1050
Roland, my friend, it's time to sound your horn;
King Charles will hear, and bring his army back."
Roland replies, "You must think I've gone mad!
In all sweet France I'd forfeit my good name!
No! I will strike great blows with Durendal,
Crimson the blade up to the hilt of gold.
To those foul pagans I promise bitter woe—
They all are doomed to die at Roncevaux!"   AOI

LXXXIV

"Roland, my friend, let the Oliphant sound!
King Charles will hear it, his host will all turn back,   1060
His valiant barons will help us in this fight."
Roland replies, "Almighty God forbid
That I bring shame upon my family,
And cause sweet France to fall into disgrace!
I'll strike that horde with my good Durendal;
My sword is ready, girded here at my side,
And soon you'll see its keen blade dripping blood.
The Saracens will curse the evil day
They challenged us, for we will make them pay."   AOI

LXXXV

"Roland, my friend, I **pray** you, sound your horn!   1070
King Charlemagne, crossing the mountain pass,
Won't fail, I swear it, to bring back all his Franks."
"May God forbid!" Count Roland answers then.
"No man on earth shall have the right to say

1059. Oliphant, that is, made of ivory.

That I for pagans   sounded the Oliphant!
I will not bring   my family to shame.
I'll fight this battle;   my Durendal shall strike
A thousand blows   and seven hundred more;
You'll see bright blood   flow from the blade's keen steel.
1080   We have good men;   their prowess will prevail,
And not one Spaniard   shall live to tell the tale."

LXXXVI

Oliver says,   "Never would you be blamed;
I've seen the pagans,   the Saracens of Spain.
They fill the valleys,   cover the mountain peaks;
On every hill,   and every wide-spread plain,
Vast hosts assemble   from that alien race;
Our company   numbers but very few."
Roland replies,   "The better, then, we'll fight!
If it please God   and His angelic host,
1090   I won't betray   the glory of sweet France!
Better to die   than learn to live with shame—
Charles loves us more   as our keen swords win fame."

LXXXVII

Roland's a hero,   and Oliver is wise;
Both are so brave   men marvel at their deeds.
When they mount chargers,   take up their swords and shields,
Not death itself   could drive them from the field.
They are good men;   their words are fierce and proud.
With wrathful speed   the pagans ride to war.
Oliver says,   "Roland, you see them now.
1100   They're very close,   the king too far away.
You were too proud   to sound the Oliphant:
If Charles were with us,   we would not come to grief.
Look up above us,   close to the Gate of Spain:
There stands the guard—   who would not pity them!

To fight this battle   means not to fight again."
Roland replies,   "Don't speak so foolishly!
Cursed be the heart   that cowers in the breast!
We'll hold our ground;   if they will meet us here,
Our foes will find us   ready with sword and spear."   AOI

LXXXVIII

When Roland sees   the fight will soon begin,   *1110*
Lions and leopards   are not so fierce as he.
Calling the Franks,   he says to Oliver:
"Noble companion,   my friend, don't talk that way!
The Emperor Charles,   who left us in command
Of twenty thousand   he chose to guard the pass,
Made very sure   no coward's in their ranks.
In his lord's service   a man must suffer pain,
Bitterest cold   and burning heat endure;
He must be willing   to lose his flesh and blood.
Strike with your lance,   and I'll wield Durendal—   *1120*
The king himself   presented it to me—
And if I die,   whoever takes my sword
Can say its master   has nobly served his lord."

LXXXIX

Archbishop Turpin   comes forward then to speak.
He spurs his horse   and gallops up a hill,
Summons the Franks,   and preaches in these words:
"My noble lords,   Charlemagne left us here,
And may our deaths   do honor to the king!
Now you must help   defend our holy Faith!

1105. Jenkins interprets this line to mean that the men of the guard
are themselves *dolente*, sorrowful.
1123. The word "vassal" in this context does seem to refer to Roland's
relationship with his liege-lord, but elsewhere, as in line 1094, it refers
primarily to the characteristics of a good vassal, particularly valor.

1130 War is upon us— I need not tell you that—
Before your eyes   you see the Saracens.
Confess your sins,   ask God to pardon you;
I'll grant you absolution   to save your souls.
Your deaths would be   a holy martyrdom,
And you'll have places   in highest Paradise."
The French dismount;   they kneel upon the ground.
Then the archbishop,   blessing them in God's name,
Told them, for penance,   to strike when battle came.

XC

The kneeling Franks   have risen to their feet.
1140 They are absolved,   and free from any sin;
Archbishop Turpin   has signed them with the cross.
Now they have mounted   swift horses bred for war;
They bear the weapons   befitting them as knights.
Thus they await   the Saracen attack.
Count Roland calls   Oliver to his side:
"My lord companion,   the words you spoke were true;
This is the work   of faithless Ganelon—
He sold us all   for treasure, gold and coins.
Now may he suffer   the emperor's revenge!
1150 As for the bargain   that King Marsile has made,
Without good swords   he'll forfeit what he paid." AOI

XCI

At Roncevaux   Count Roland passes by,
Riding his charger,   swift-running Veillantif.
He's armed for battle,   splendid in shining mail.
As he parades,   he brandishes his lance,
Turning the point   straight up against the sky,
And from the spearhead   a banner flies, pure white,

1152. "At Roncevaux," that is, *as porz d'Espaigne*—the pass, the "gates
of Spain."

With long gold fringes   that beat against his hands.
Fair to behold,   he laughs, serene and gay.
Now close behind him   comes Oliver, his friend,   1160
With all the Frenchmen   cheering their mighty lord.
Fiercely his eyes   confront the Saracens;
Humbly and gently   he gazes at the Franks,
Speaking to them   with gallant courtesy:
"Barons, my lords,   softly now, keep the pace!
Here come the pagans   looking for martyrdom.
We'll have such plunder   before the day is out,
As no French king   has ever won before!"
And at this moment   the armies join in war.   AOI

XCII

Oliver says,   "I have no heart for words.   1170
You were too proud   to sound the Oliphant:
No help at all   you'll have from Charlemagne.
It's not his fault—   he doesn't know our plight,
Nor will the men   here with us be to blame.
But now, ride on,   to fight as you know how.
Barons, my lords,   in battle hold your ground!
And in God's name,   I charge you, be resolved
To strike great blows   for those you have to take.
Let's not forget   the war-cry of King Charles!"
He says these words,   and all the Franks cry out;   1180
No one who heard   that mighty shout, "Montjoie!"
Would soon forget   the valor of these men.

1158. The text does not permit editors to guarantee the long gold
fringes on Roland's banner, but they are possible, and certainly in
the proper spirit.
1161. That is, acclaim him as their *guarant*, protector.
1174. This line could equally well mean: "Nor will the men with
Charles be to blame."
1181. "Montjoie"—the poet of the *Roland* explains its origin (2503–
11, 3094–5). Jenkins suggests also the pilgrims' cry of joy on seeing
the end of their quest for Monte Gaudia or a similar hill near
Jerusalem or Santiago, but no sure explanation exists.

And then, how fiercely, God! they begin to ride,
Spurring their horses to give their utmost speed,
They race to strike— what else is there to do?
The Saracens stand firm; they won't retreat.
Pagans and Christians, behold! in battle meet.

XCIII

King Marsile's nephew, Aelroth is his name,
First of the pagans, rides out before the host,
1190 Taunting our Franks with loud malicious words:
"Today, foul Frenchmen, you'll break a lance with us;
You stand here now abandoned and betrayed!
The king was mad to leave you at the pass:
This day sweet France will see its pride cast down.
The Emperor Charles will lose his good right arm!"
Count Roland hears him, God! with what pain and rage!
He spurs his horse to run with all its might,
Levels his lance, strikes Aelroth such a blow
His shield is shattered, the hauberk split in two,
1200 The pagan's bones crack open in his chest,
His broken spine sticks out behind his back
So that the spear drives out his very soul.
Under the thrust the body starts to fall,
And Roland hurls him a spear's length from his horse;
He falls down dead, his neck broken in two.
But still Count Roland gives him these parting words:
"Foul infidel, King Charles is not a fool,
Nor was he ever unfaithful to his trust.
Wisely he chose that we should guard the pass;
1210 Sweet France will lose no glory here today.
Strike on, you Franks! First blood will win the fight!
Their cause is evil, and we are in the right." AOI

XCIV

A duke is there whose name is Falsaron,
Aelroth's uncle, brother to King Marsile:

Dathan was his, and he held Abiron—
No man more ruthless was ever seen on earth.
He was a giant: his forehead, monstrous wide,
A good six inches measured from eye to eye.
Because he grieves to see his nephew dead,
He rushes forward to challenge any foe,   *1220*
All the while shouting the pagan battle cry.
In his great fury he challenges the Franks:
"Today sweet France will see its honor fall!"
Oliver hears this, and mightily enraged,
Pricking his horse with spurs of shining gold,
Charges to strike him, as a true knight would do.
The shield cracks open, the hauberk splits apart,
Up to the pennon the spear-head drives on through;
Thrust from his saddle, Falsaron hits the ground.
The count looks down to see the scoundrel die,   *1230*
And speaks to him in proud and fiery words:
"You know now, felon, how much I heed your threats!
Strike on, you Franks! They've come here to be slain."
"Montjoie!" he shouts, the cry of Charlemagne. AOI

XCV

A king is there, his name is Corsalis,
From Barbary, that land across the sea.
He shouts this counsel to cheer the Saracens:
"Here is a battle easy enough to win—
When so few Franks are left to guard the pass
What can we do but hold them in contempt?   *1240*
Charles has no power to save a single one:
This is the day when they are doomed to die."
Archbishop Turpin has heard him make this boast;
In all the world he hates no man so much.
Pricking his horse with spurs of purest gold,

1221. The text does not give us the words of the pagan war-cry.
1226. The expression *en guise de baron* occurs very often in the text,
and would seem to be simply a more picturesque way of saying
"valiantly." See also 1889 and 1902.

He strikes the Berber   such a tremendous blow
His shield splits open,   the chain-mail flies apart,
Turpin's great spear   comes out beyond his back,
And falling backward   under that awful thrust,
1250   Corsalis lands   a spear's length from his horse.
Turpin looks back,   and sees that vile wretch die,
Nor will he leave   before he tells him this:
"Foul infidel,   you made your boast with lies.
Who serves King Charles   is ever safe from harm,
And of our Franks   not one would wish to flee.
All your companions   will soon be put to rest.
I've news for you—   there's no way out but death.
Strike, men of France!   Forget not who you are!
Thanks be to God,   first blood is on our side."
1260   And then "Montjoie!"   to claim the field, he cried.

XCVI

Count Gerin strikes   Malprimes de Brigal
Whose great stout shield   proves not worth half a cent:
The blow, dead center,   shatters the crystal boss,
And half the shield   goes crashing to the ground;
Right through the hauberk   the heavy spearhead thrusts,
Pierces the flesh,   and lodges deep inside.
The wretched pagan   falls in a crumpled heap;
A devil carries   his soul away to keep.   AOI

XCVII

Then the emir   is struck by Gerier
1270   Who breaks his shield   and shatters his chain-mail,
Pierces his body   with a great thrust of steel
Until the spearhead   comes out the other side.
Balaguer falls   a spear's length from his horse.
Oliver says,   "Valor will beat their force!"

1269. That is, the Emir of Balaguer.

XCVIII

Moriane's emir   receives Duke Samson's charge;
Flowers and gold   will not defend his shield,
Nor will his chain-mail   do him a bit of good.
His heart cut open,   his liver and his lungs,
He falls down dead,   if any care or no.
Says the archbishop, "That was a baron's blow!"   *1280*

XCIX

Then Anseïs   charges on his swift horse;
When his spear strikes   Torgis of Tortelose,
The shield cracks open   below the golden boss,
The double hauberk   splits open, snaps apart,
The spearhead thrusts   into the pagan's flesh
Until the point   comes out beyond his back.
Torgis falls dead,   face down upon the field.
Count Roland says,   "That was a hero's deed."

C

The Gascon knight,   Engelier de Bordeaux,
Spurs on his horse,   and lets him have his head,   *1290*
Charging to strike   Escremiz de Valterne;
He cracks the shield   hung round the pagan's neck,
Pierces the hauberk   just where the flap is laced,
Thrusts through his chest   between the collarbones,
And fells him dead   a spear's length from his horse.
Engelier says, "For death you set your course." AOI

CI

Then Oton strikes   the pagan Estorgans,
Hitting his shield   hard on the upper edge,

1280. The noun *ber*, oblique *baron*, is used nonspecifically to refer
to a nobleman or a hero.

He cuts its quarters,   the crimson and the white;
1300   The hauberk cracks   where the two halves are joined,
The shining spear-point   thrusts deep into his flesh.
Thrown from his charger,   he lies dead on the ground,
And Oton says,   "See who will save you now!"

CII

Then Berengier   charges Estramariz,
Shatters his spear,   splits the chain-mail apart;
He drives his spear-point   deep through the pagan's flesh,
Fells him among   a thousand Saracens.
The Franks have killed   ten of the pagan peers;
These two alone   have not come to defeat:
1310   One is Chernuble,   the other Margariz.

CIII

That valiant knight,   Margariz of Seville,
Handsome and strong,   agile and very quick,
Spurs on his horse   and charges Oliver,
Piercing his shield   under its boss of gold
So that the spear-point   grazes his very ribs.
The hand of God   has turned aside that thrust,
The shaft is broken;   Oliver does not fall.
Margariz gallops on,   right through the Franks,
And blows his trumpets   to cheer the pagan ranks.

CIV

1320   Now wondrous battle   rages throughout the field.
Roland fights on,   not caring to keep safe,
Strikes with his spear   until the shaft is gone—
And fifteen blows   it gave before it broke.
Then from its scabbard   he draws great Durendal,
Spurs on and charges   Chernuble de Munigre,

Slashing his helmet   where the bright rubies gleam,
Slices his hood   and downward through his hair,
Between the eyes   he cuts his face in two,
Through the bright hauberk,   of tightly-woven mail,
And all his body   down to the groin is split;   1330
Then through the saddle   adorned with threads of gold,
The sword drives deep   into the pagan's horse,
Cleaving the spine   where there's a joint or no—
Both man and beast   fall dead in thick green grass.
Then Roland says,   "Foul serf, you've found your doom.
See how Mohammed   protects you in the fray!
No man so vile   will win this fight today."

CV

Count Roland gallops   everywhere in the field
With Durendal,   well-made to slash and cleave.
Great is the havoc   among the Saracens—   1340
One on the other   he heaps their bodies high!
The bright blood flows   streaming along the ground,
Roland's hauberk   and both his arms are red,
The neck and shoulders   of his good charger too.
Count Oliver   fights on and never stops;
The other peers,   like him, deserve all praise.
The valiant Franks   strike and cut down their foes;
The pagans die,   or stricken, fall and faint.
Says the archbishop,   "God's blessing be their thanks!"
He shouts, "Montjoie!"   the war-cry of the Franks.   AOI   1350

CVI

Oliver rides   through the thick of the fray;
His spear is shattered,   only a stump remains.

1326. The red jewels here designated as rubies are called "carbuncles"
throughout the text, a word which may have been glamorous once,
but certainly is not now. The meaning seems to be otherwise the
same: any of several red, glowing gems.

He gallops on, and charges Malsaron,
Breaking his shield bright with flowers and gold;
The pagan's eyes are thrust out of his head,
Parts of his brain stream down him to his feet,
He goes to join the seven hundred slain.
Oliver kills Torgis and Esturgoz;
The spear-shaft breaks and splinters in his hands.
1360   Then Roland says, "What are you doing, friend?
For such a battle why did you choose a stick?
I'll take my chances with iron and stout steel!
Where is your sword, the one you call Halteclere,
With crystal hilt and guard of shining gold?"
"I had no time," he says, "to draw my sword,
With all those pagans to send to their reward!" AOI

CVII

Lord Oliver has drawn his good Halteclere,
The sword that Roland was asking him to use,
And shows its powers in a most knightly way:
1370   He rides to strike Justin de Val Ferrée—
With just one blow he splits that pagan's head,
Cleaves through the body, the brightly polished mail,
The splendid saddle sparkling with gold and jewels,
And breaks the spine of Justin's war-horse too;
Both bodies fall into the meadow grass.
And Roland says, "That's my true brother now!
For such great blows Charlemagne holds us dear."
Then from all sides, "Montjoie!" the Frenchmen cheer. AOI

CVIII

Count Gerin rides a horse he calls Sorel,
1380   With Gerier, his friend, on Passecerf;
They loosen reins and spur their horses on,
Racing to charge the pagan Timozel.
One strikes the hauberk, the other hits the shield,

Both of their spears,   deep in his body, break;
He's thrown off backward,   dead, in a fallow field.
Which was the faster   of these two chevaliers?
I haven't heard,   and certainly can't tell.
Eperveris,   whose father was Borel,
Then met his slayer,   the Gascon Engelier.
Archbishop Turpin   has slaughtered Siglorel;   1390
The great enchanter   went once before to Hell—
That time by magic,   with Jupiter as guide.
Then Turpin says,   "I think he was no friend!"
And Roland answers,   "To death that villain goes.
Oliver, brother,   I love to see such blows!"

CIX

Meanwhile the battle   grows hotter all the time,
Both Franks and pagans   exchange prodigious blows;
Some charge and strike,   others defend their lives.
Spears without number   are shattered, stained with blood,
Pennons are ripped,   and battle-flags destroyed!   1400
So many Franks   who lay down their young lives
Will not return   to mothers or to wives
Or to those waiting   beyond the Gates of Spain.
King Charlemagne   will weep for bitter woe;
What good are tears?   His help will come too late.
Ill was he served   by Ganelon who went
To Saragossa   and sold the king's own men.
For that betrayal,   he lost his life and limbs;
The trial at Aix   condemned him to be hanged

1386-7. These lines are omitted by Jenkins as not genuine, and he
assumes that they refer to the horses. The two lines that follow are
his own reconstruction, approved by Bédier but not included in his
text.
1392. Jenkins points out that Jupiter, like Apollo in line 8, is a
demon. But the latter is worshiped as a god, if only by the Saracens.
Classical nomenclature in the *Roland* is no more reliable than the
poet's geography.

1410   With thirty kinsmen   who also had to pay,
And never thought   their lives would end that way.   AOI

CX

Now fierce and grim   the battle rages on.
Oliver, Roland—   how valiantly they fight!
Turpin delivers   more than a thousand blows;
Among the peers   none dreams of holding back,
And all together,   the Franks, as one man, strike.
By hundreds, thousands,   the pagans fall and die;
There's no way out   except for those who flee:
Each one who stays   is living his last day.
1420   But others die—   the best among the Franks—
They'll never see   their families, their wives,
Or Charlemagne   who waits beyond the pass.
A fearful storm   that very day strikes France;
Through rushing winds   long peals of thunder roar,
And heavy rains,   enormous hailstones fall,
Great bolts of lightning   are striking everywhere.
Now the whole earth   is trembling dreadfully
From Saint Michel   all the way down to Seinz,
From Besançon   to Wissant on the sea;
1430   There is no stronghold   without a shattered wall.
At noontime shadows   darken the light of day;
The only brightness   comes when the black sky cracks,
And no man sees it   who isn't terrified.
Many declare,   "The world is at an end—
The Day of Wrath   has come upon us now!"
But they know nothing,   and they believe a lie.
The heavens grieve   that Roland is to die.

CXI

The Franks of France   have struck with mighty force;
Enormous numbers   of Saracens are slain:
1440   A hundred thousand,   and just one man remains.

1440. The one remaining pagan is presumably Margariz.

Says the archbishop,   "Our Franks are brave and true;
In all the world   there are no better men.
Gesta Francorum   says of our emperor
That he was served   by heroes one and all."
They walk the field,   searching among the dead;
For grief and pity   they cannot help but weep,
Thinking of those   whose loved ones won't come back.
Then King Marsile   launches a new attack. AOI

CXII

Now King Marsile   through a deep valley rides
With the great host   he summoned to his aid: 1450
Twenty battalions   march with the Saracen.
Their helmets gleam   with gold and precious stones,
Bright are their shields,   their hauberks saffron-gold.
With seven hundred trumpets   sounding the charge,
Their coming echoes   for many miles around.
Then Roland says,   "Oliver, brother, friend,
Foul Ganelon   has sent us to our deaths;
But this betrayal   can never be concealed,
And we can leave   our vengence to King Charles.
We'll have a battle   to try our utmost strength—   1460
Fiercer than any   the world has seen before.
I'll strike them down   with Durendal, my sword,
And you, companion,   strike with your own Halteclere.
We've carried them   through so many far lands,
So many battles   we've won thanks to these blades!
No evil songs   to mock them shall be made." AOI

CXIII

King Marsile sees   the slaughter of his men.
Then horns and trumpets   ring out at his command,

1443. What exactly was said in the *Gesta Francorum* ("Deeds of the
Franks") is most uncertain. Bédier considered line 1444 a *locus
desperatus*; the present translation follows Jenkins.

And he rides on   with his assembled host.
1470 One Saracen   rides out in front: Abisme,
The fiercest man   in all that company.
Evil at heart,   and guilty of great crimes,
He has no faith   in Mary's holy Son.
This pagan's skin   is black as melted pitch.
He'd rather murder   or do vile treachery
Than have the gift   of all Galicia's gold.
He never laughs   or joins in any sport,
But he is bold   and valiant when he fights.
This makes him dear   to the foul king Marsile;
1480 He bears the dragon,   flag of the Saracens.
Archbishop Turpin   will be no friend to him—
Seeing this pagan,   he longs to strike him down.
In a low voice   he speaks thus to himself:
"This man must be   a mighty heretic—
Surely his death   has been too long delayed.
I have no love   for men who are afraid."

CXIV

And so the battle   begins with Turpin's charge.
He rides a horse   he took from King Grossaille,
That time in Denmark   he fought him to his death.
1490 The horse is swift   and spirited and proud;
His hooves are hollow,   slender and strong his legs,
Short in the thigh,   his quarters large around,
His chest is deep,   his back set straight and high.
White is his tail,   yellow his flowing mane,
His ears are small,   his head of tawny gold;
No charger set   to race him has a chance.
Archbishop Turpin   spurs on against Abisme—
And with what valor!   Nothing can stop him now.

1486. That is, "I never loved a coward or cowardice"; but it seems
clear that Turpin refers to himself, feeling perhaps even a bit reluctant
to attack so dreadful a Saracen.

He strikes the shield   a superhuman blow;
Its surface sparkles   with topaz, amethyst,   1500
Stones of great virtue,   rubies that hotly glow—
(In Val Metas   a devil gave that shield
To the emir,   who gave it to Abisme).
But Turpin's spear   accords it no respect:
After his blow   it isn't worth a cent.
Right through that pagan   his spear thrusts like a spit;
He throws the body   into an empty space.
The Frenchmen say,   "Against him no one stands!
The holy staff   is safe in Turpin's hands."

CXV

The Franks can see   that hosts of Saracens   1510
All through the field   advance on every side.
They cry out often   to Roland, Oliver,
The twelve French peers,   to come to their defense.
Archbishop Turpin   counsels them in this way:
"Barons, my lords,   surrender not to fear,
But in God's name,   I pray you, hold your ground,
That no man mock you   in a malicious song—
Better to die   with honor on this field!
Very soon now   we'll meet our promised end;
We cannot hope   to live beyond today.   1520
But this I tell you   is true without a doubt:
For you stand open   the gates of Paradise:
You'll take your places   beside the Innocents."
Hearing these words,   the Frenchmen all rejoice;
"Montjoie!" they cry,   as with a single voice. AOI

1501. "Stones of great virtue" comes from a suggestion of Jenkins and
from the otherwise uncertain identification of *esterminals*.
1503. The emir is Galafe.
1519. This has been interpreted, I think incorrectly, as a reference to the
Day of Judgment.

CXVI

From Saragossa   there came a Saracen
Who called his own   one-half of all that town.
This Climborin,   who was no perfect knight,
Heard the count's oath   that he'd betray the Franks,
1530 In sign of friendship   kissed the count on the mouth,
And gave him gifts: his helm, a precious stone.
Climborin says   he'll bring the Empire down,
And strike the crown   from Charlemagne's proud head.
He rides a charger   whose name is Barbamosche—
No hawk or swallow   can fly as fast as he.
The pagan spurs,   and gives the horse his head,
Charging to strike   the Gascon Engelier.
Hauberk and shield   cannot protect him now;
Climborin's thrust   goes deep into his flesh
1540 Until the spear-head   comes out the other side.
He flings the body   a spear's length from his horse,
And then he shouts,   "They're asking for defeat!
Strike them down, pagans—   destroy them in their ranks!"
"There died a hero.   God save us!" cry the Franks.   AOI

CXVII

And then Count Roland   calls Oliver aside:
"My lord, companion,   Engelier has been slain;
We cannot boast   a better knight than he."
The count replies,   "God grant me his revenge!"
With golden spurs   he urges on his horse,
1550 Holding aloft   Halteclere all red with blood;
With mighty force   he strikes at Climborin,
Pulls out his sword—   the Saracen falls dead,
And demons come   to carry off his soul.
Oliver kills   Duke Alphaïen next,
Then Escababi   is parted from his head.
The count unhorses   seven more Arab knights

Who won't be fit ever to fight again.
And Roland says, "Now wrathful grows my friend!
His deeds of valor don't shrink beside my own!
For blows like that Charles' love is our reward." 1560
And then he shouts, "Strike on, you noble lords!"

CXVIII

There was a pagan whose name was Valdabron.
He raised to knighthood the Saracen Marsile.
Four hundred galleys he rules upon the sea,
And every sailor is bound by oath to him.
His treachery once took Jerusalem,
He desecrated Solomon's Temple there—
Close to the fonts he killed the patriarch.
To Ganelon, who promised him good faith,
He gave his sword and then a thousand coins. 1570
He rides a horse whose name is Gramimond—
There is no falcon who'd beat him in a race.
Urging him now with the sharp prick of spurs,
Valdabron charges Samson, the mighty duke;
He breaks his shield, the hauberk splits in two,
Up to the pennon he thrusts the spear-point through,
And fells the duke a spear's length from his horse:
"Strike them down, pagans, these Franks don't have a chance!"
"There died a hero," say grieving men of France. AOI

CXIX

As for Count Roland, when he sees Samson dead, 1580
You can imagine the sorrow that he feels.

1559. This line has been much discussed, since it seems ungracious if
taken literally. I think it is a litotes, like the preceding line, although
Roland was never modest (see 791), nor was boasting considered
bad manners in his time.
1563. In Jenkins' edition, unlike Bédier's, line 618 is corrected to be
similar to this, and in both instances *levat* is taken to mean "act as
godfather to."

He spurs his horse   and charges with great speed,
Holding his sword   worth more than purest gold.
Valiant, he strikes   with every ounce of strength
Valdabron's helmet   sparkling with precious stones,
Splits his head open,   his body cased in mail;
Cleaving the saddle,   gilded and set with jewels:
The blade goes deeper   and breaks the horse's back.
Some cheer, some grieve,   but man and beast fall dead.
1590   The pagans say,   "You've struck us a hard blow!"
And Roland answers,   "Why should I love your side?
You're in the wrong,   and you are full of pride." AOI

CXX

From Africa   there came an African
Called Malquiant,   the son of King Malcud.
His arms and armor,   all overlaid with gold,
Gleam in the sunlight,   the brightest on the field.
He sits a charger   whose name is Saut-Perdu—
No horse can win   against him in a race.
Malquiant strikes   the fiery Anseïs,
1600   Smashing to bits   the blue and crimson shield;
The hauberk breaks   where it was joined in two,
Spear-point and shaft   into the body thrust:
The count is dead;   his time has all run through.
The French lords say,   "Baron, we grieve for you!"

CXXI

Now through the battle   Archbishop Turpin rides:
No tonsured priest   who ever sang a mass
Had such high courage   to do heroic deeds.
This, to the pagan: "God smite you with His curse!
You have cut down   a man my heart laments."
1610   He sends his horse   galloping on to charge,
Strikes Malquiant   through his Toledo shield,
And flings his body   onto the grassy field.

CXXII

And then comes forward   a pagan called Grandoine,
Capuel's son,   he's Cappadocia's heir.
He sits a horse   whose name is Marmorie—
It gallops faster   than any bird can fly.
He loosens reins   and pricks him with his spurs
To charge Count Gerin   with all his skill and force.
The crimson shield   falls from the Frenchman's neck,
His hauberk breaks,   most of it splits away,   *1620*
Then the blue banner   thrusts deep into his flesh,
And Grandoine hurls   his body to a rock.
That pagan kills   Gerin's friend Gerier,
And Bérengier,   and Gui de Saint-Antoine;
He charges next   the mighty duke Austorge,
Lord of Valence   and Envers on the Rhône,
Who falls down dead   as all the pagans cheer.
The Frenchmen say,   "Our end is coming near."

CXXIII

Roland holds high   his sword stained red with blood.
He has not missed   the outcry of the Franks,   *1630*
And feels such sorrow   he thinks his heart will break.
This, to the pagan: "God's curse upon you fall!
I'll sell you dear   the noble lord you've slain!"
He spurs his horse   who cares not to delay,
Seeks out Grandoine,   hoping to make him pay.

CXXIV

Grandoine is valiant,   powerful, very brave;
He is a hero,   bold on the battlefield.
All of a sudden   Count Roland bars his path.
Although the pagan   never saw him before,
By his proud face   he knows him, by his eyes,   *1640*

His noble bearing,   his stature, tall and strong;
Grandoine can't help   but tremble with great fear.
He tries to flee,   but cannot get away
Before Count Roland   stops him with such a blow
That his whole helmet   down to the nose-piece breaks,
The sword blade cleaves   through nose and mouth and teeth,
Down through his body   encased in shining mail,
Into the saddle   all silver-trimmed and gold,
And drives on deep   into the horse's back.
1650 Nothing can save them—   both man and beast fall dead.
Spaniards cry out   in horror at the sight.
The Frenchmen say,   "Our lord knows how to fight!"

CXXV

The wondrous battle   is spirited and grim;
Blow after blow   the angry Frenchmen strike.
Their sword blades cleave   through fists and ribs and spines,
Through cloth and armor   into the living flesh.
On the green grass   the bright blood flows in streams.
The pagans say,   "This is too much for us!
Mohammed's curse   upon the Empire fall!
1660 There are no men   as hard to kill as these."
And to Marsile   the Saracens cry out:
"Ride to our aid,   or we'll be put to rout!"

CXXVI

The battle grows   ever more swift and fierce.
The Frenchmen strike   keen blows with burnished spears.
You would have seen   so many in great pain,
So many dead,   so many drenched in blood!
Face up or downward,   one on the other lies.

1658. This line is supplied by most editors. Bédier omits it, both in
his text and in his translation, without indication.

The Saracens   cannot bear any more:
They flee the field,   whether they will or no.
The wrathful Franks   pursue them as they go.   AOI   1670

CXXVII

Count Roland says   to Oliver his friend:
"My lord companion,   I'm sure you will agree
That our archbishop   makes a most valiant knight—
There is none better   on earth beneath the sky;
With lance in hand,   or spear, how he can fight!"
The count replies,   "Then let's go to his side!"
When he has spoken,   the Franks attack once more.
Hard are the blows,   the slaughter pitiless;
Many a Christian   is brought to grievous pain.
Then to behold   Roland and Oliver   1680
Wielding their swords   to cut the pagans down!
Beside them Turpin   thrusts with his mighty spear.
We know what happened   according to the *Geste*,
Chronicles, records   bear witness to the fact:
Four thousand pagans   by those few Franks were slain.
Through four assaults   the Frenchmen hold their ground.
But with the fifth   their strength comes to an end.
That final charge   kills all the knights of France
Except for sixty   who by God's will survive—
They'll make the pagans   pay dearly for their lives!   AOI   1690

CXXVIII

Count Roland sees   the slaughter of the Franks.
He says these words   to Oliver his friend:
"Noble companion,   what do you counsel now?
So many Franks   lie dead upon the field—
Well could we weep   for that fair land, sweet France,
Which will not see   these valiant lords again.
Oh! Charles, my friend,   if only you were here!

Oliver, brother,   how can we call him back?
Is there no way   to tell the king our plight?"
1700   Oliver answers, "Not if we save our fame.
Better to die   than learn to live with shame."   AOI

CXXIX

Then Roland says,   "I'll sound the Oliphant.
King Charles will hear it   on the high mountain pass;
I promise you,   the Franks will all turn back."
Oliver answers, "Then you would bring disgrace
And such dishonor   on your whole family
The shame of it   would last them all their lives.
Three times I asked,   and you would not agree;
You still can do it,   but not with my consent.
1710   To sound the horn   denies your valor now.
And both your arms   are red with blood of foes!"
The count replies, "I've struck some pretty blows."   AOI

CXXX

Then Roland says,   "This has become a war.
I'll blow my horn,   and Charlemagne will hear."
Oliver says, "Then you'll disgrace your name.
Each time I asked you,   companion, you refused.
If Charles were with us,   we would not come to grief.
No one can say   our Franks have been to blame.
I promise you—   I swear it by my beard—
1720   If I should live   to see my sister's face,
You'll never lie   in Alda's sweet embrace!"   AOI

CXXXI

Then says the count, "You're angry at me. Why?"
Oliver answers, "Roland, you are to blame.
There is no madness   in courage for good cause,

1698. But Jenkins: "How can we fight them now?" Jenkins' translation
of *lo faire* throughout as referring to battle seems to me very difficult
to defend.

But men should listen to reason, not blind pride.
You were too reckless, and so these Franks have died.
Never again will we serve Charlemagne.
Had you believed me, my lord would be here now,
We would have fought and beat the Saracens,
Marsile would be our prisoner, or dead. 1730
We are the victims of your great prowess now!
We won't be there, alas! to help King Charles,
A man whose peer will not be seen on earth.
And you will die, leaving sweet France to shame.
Brothers in arms we've been until this day;
Now we have only a last farewell to say." AOI

CXXXII

Archbishop Turpin, hearing their angry words,
Urges his horse with spurs made of pure gold,
And riding up, reproaches both of them:
"Roland, my lord, and you, Lord Oliver, 1740
End your dispute, I pray you, in God's name.
It's too late now to blow the horn for help,
But just the same, that's what you'd better do.
If the king comes, at least we'll be avenged—
Why should the Spaniards go home safe to rejoice?
And then the Franks will ride back to this place;
They'll find us dead, our bodies hacked by swords,
Put us in coffins carried on horses' backs,
And they will weep for pity and for grief.
We will be buried with honor in a church, 1750
And not be eaten by wolves and pigs and dogs."
Then Roland answers: "Your words are wise, my lord."

1731. *Vostre proecce, Rollant, mar la veïmes!* The use of *mare* in
this sense, it seems to me, should not be translated so as to imply
an absolute condemnation. Oliver, even in fury, would hardly regret
the whole experience of Roland's valor, but rather would lament that
so much valor should come to so unfortunate an end (similarly, line
1860). The same considerations apply when *mare* is used with *estre,* as
in *Barun, tant mare fus!* (line 1604), or *Tant mar fustes hardiz!*
(line 2027).

CXXXIII

Count Roland presses   the horn against his mouth;
He grasps it hard,   and sounds a mighty blast.
High are the hills,   that great voice reaches far—
They hear it echo   full thirty leagues around.
Charlemagne hears,   and so do all his men.
The Emperor says,   "Our Franks are in a fight!"
Count Ganelon   returns a swift reply:
1760 "Except from you,   I'd take that for a lie!"   AOI

CXXXIV

And now Count Roland,   in anguish and in pain,
With all his strength   sounds the great horn again.
Bright drops of blood   are springing from his mouth,
Veins in his forehead   are cracking with the strain.
That mighty voice   cries out a second time;
Charlemagne hears it,   high on the mountain pass,
Duke Naimon listens,   and so do all the Franks.
Then says the king,   "That is Count Roland's horn!
He'd never sound it,   except for an attack."
1770 Ganelon says,   "What battle can there be?
You have grown old,   your hair is streaked with white;
The words you speak   could well befit a child.
You ought to know   how great is Roland's pride—
The wonder is   God suffers it so long.
He captured Noples,   and not by your command,
And then flushed out   the Saracens inside;
He fought them all,   Roland, your loyal man,
And then took water   and washed the field of blood,
Hoping that you   would not detect the fight.
1780 Just for a rabbit   he'll blow his horn all day!
Now he is playing   some game to please his peers.
Who in the world   would dare make war on him!
Ride on, I tell you!   What are we waiting for?
We've far to go   to see our lands once more."   AOI

CXXXV

Count Roland's mouth   is crimson with his blood,
His temples broken   by the tremendous strain.
He sounds the horn   in anguish and in pain.
Charlemagne hears,   and so do all the Franks.
Then says the king,   "How long that horn resounds!"
Duke Naimon answers,   "Great valor swells the sound!   *1790*
Roland is fighting: he must have been betrayed—
And by that man   who tells you to hang back.
Take up your arms,   let your war-cry ring out!
Your household needs you,   now speed to its defense.
You've heard enough   how Roland's horn laments!"

CXXXVI

The Emperor Charles   orders his horns to sound.
The French dismount,   prepare themselves for war.
They put on hauberks,   helmets and golden swords;
Their shields are good,   heavy their spears and strong,
Their battle-flags   are crimson, blue and white.   *1800*
Riding their chargers,   the barons of the host
Spur on and gallop   back through the mountain pass.
Each to the other   pronounces this same vow:
"When we get there,   if Roland's still alive,
We'll fight beside him,   striking hard blows and straight."
What does it matter?   Their help will come too late.

CXXXVII

All afternoon   the sun shines bright and clear,
Armor and weapons   are gleaming in the light,
Hauberks and helmets   glitter as if on fire,
And all the shields,   brilliant with painted flowers,   *1810*
And all the spears   and gilded battle flags.
In bitter wrath   the Emperor rides on,
The men of France,   in sorrow and in rage.

There is not one   who can hold back his tears;
Because of Roland,   the Frenchmen are afraid.
King Charles commands   that Ganelon be seized;
Summoning forth   all of his household cooks,
He tells their chief,   Besgon, what should be done:
"Here is a felon   I'm leaving in your charge—
1820   He has betrayed   the vassals of my house."
The cook takes over;   a hundred kitchen boys,
The best and worst,   will guard Count Ganelon.
They pluck the hairs   from his moustache and beard,
Each with his fist   strikes him four mighty blows,
And then they beat him   with heavy sticks and clubs.
An iron collar   is put around his neck,
And then they chain him   as if he were a bear.
On a mule's back,   trussed up, he will remain.
They'll guard him well,   and wait for Charlemagne.   AOI

CXXXVIII

1830   High are the hills,   and shadowy and vast,
Deep the defiles,   and swift the mountain streams.
The trumpets sound   ahead and to the rear,
Blaring replies   to Roland's Oliphant.
In bitter wrath   the Emperor rides on,
The men of France   in sorrow and in rage;
Not one but grieves   and bitterly laments,
Praying that God   will keep Count Roland safe
Until they come   and join him in the field—
How they will fight   when they are at his side!
1840   What does it matter   how loyally they strive?
They'll be too late   whenever they arrive.   AOI

CXXXIX

Now Charlemagne   rides on in his great rage;
His beard, defiant,   outside his hauberk lies.

The lords of France   spur for the utmost speed,
There isn't one   but angrily laments
That they can't be   already on the field
Where Roland fights   against the Saracens.
I think his wound   won't let him long survive,
But God! the sixty   still fighting at his side—
No king or chieftain   has ever had their like. AOI   *1850*

CXL

Count Roland sees   the mountains and the hills
Where all around him   the Franks are lying dead;
He weeps for them,   as a true knight would do.
"Barons, my lords,   may God forgive your sins,
And grant your souls   a place in Paradise,
On holy flowers   may you forever rest!
I've never seen   vassals better than you;
You followed me   so loyally and long,
For Charlemagne   we've won such mighty lands!
The king's own household,   alas! brings him to woe.   *1860*
And that fair country   where it is sweet to live
Today laid waste   and cruelly bereaved!
Barons of France,   because of me you die;
I can't protect you,   I cannot keep you safe:
Look now to God   who never failed a trust.
Oliver, brother,   I'll not break faith with you.
I'll die of grief,   if not by pagan spears.
My lord, companion,   there's still work for us here!"

1846. *Rollant le cataigne* is usually translated "captain," but "chieftain"
is surely more accurate.
1863. The crucial words *pur mei* must certainly be understood as
"because of me" rather than "for my sake." It would be not only
presumptuous but inaccurate for Roland to say that the Franks were
dying for his sake, and the whole passage expresses his new humility—he
admits that he cannot protect his men. It is now that he truly understands why Oliver was so angry. He feels not only sorrow but remorse.

CXLI

Roland has gone   back to the battlefield.
1870   With Durendal   he strikes heroic blows:
Faldrun de Pui   he cuts down first of all,
Then twenty-four   of the best pagan knights.
No man has ever   wanted revenge so much.
Just as the stag   runs to escape the hounds,
So do the pagans   before Count Roland flee.
Says the archbishop, "Bravely you fight, and well!
Yours is the spirit   a chevalier must have,
If he bears arms   and has a horse to ride:
A man in battle   ought to be fierce and strong—
1880   For one who isn't,   I wouldn't give two cents.
Instead of fighting   let him become a monk
And spend his days   praying for all our sins."
Roland replies, "Strike on, and spare not one!"
With that the Franks   begin to fight once more.
Many a Christian   falls to the pagan swords.

CXLII

A man who knows   all captives will be slain
In such a battle   fights to the end of strength;
And so the Franks   like lions face their foes.
Behold Marsile: as a true knight would do,
1890   He sits the horse   that he has named Gaignon,
Pricks with sharp spurs,   and rides against Bevon,

1881–2. Tavernier and Jenkins believe that this passage does not necessarily imply that cloistered monks are inferior to good knights. Such an interpretation would seem to me possible only if one considered that in the heat of battle Turpin spoke more emphatically than he normally would in describing the categories of worthy activities.
1888. It is customary to indicate that this is the only formal simile in the poem.
1890. Marsile's horse is called Watchdog.

The lord of Beaune   and also of Dijon;
He breaks his shield,   the hauberk splits in two—
With that one blow   he fells the Frenchman dead.
Then Marsile kills   Ivoire and Ivon too,
And with them dies   Gérard of Roussillon.
Seeing that, Roland,   who isn't far away,
Says to the pagan,   "God smite you with His curse!
To you I owe   these good companions slain—
Nor shall we part   before that debt is paid!   *1900*
Now is the time   to teach you my sword's name."
With that he charges   as a true knight would do;
The count's keen sword   cuts off Marsile's right hand,
Then Jurfaleu   surrenders his blond head—
He was a prince,   the son of King Marsile.
The pagans cry,   "Mohammed help us now!
Gods of our country,   give us revenge on Charles,
For he has sent   such felons here to fight
That death itself   can't drive them from the field."
They tell each other,   "Let's get away from here!"   *1910*
A hundred thousand   run from the French attack;
Whoever calls,   they won't be coming back.

CXLIII

What does it matter   that King Marsile has fled?
They still must fight   his uncle Marganice,
The lord of Carthage,   Alfrere, and Garmalie,
That land accursed   called Ethiopia
Whose black men serve   as Marganice commands.
They have big noses,   their ears stick out too far;
Some fifty thousand   have come to fight the Franks.
They gallop boldly,   and in wild fury charge,   *1920*
Shouting the war-cry   dear to the pagan hosts.

1901. Thus it is apparent that the name "Durendal" has significance,
but nothing further can be effectively said on the subject.
1914. Marganice, that is, the Caliph.

Then Roland says, "Here we'll win martyrdom.
Now I can see   how little time is left;
But cursed be he   who lets his life go cheap!
Strike them, my lords,   strike with your shining swords!
Give them a battle   whether you live or die,
That none may say   we brought sweet France to shame.
When Charlemagne   comes to this battlefield,
He'll see the hosts   of slaughtered Saracens—
1930   For each of us   some fifteen pagans dead;
Charles won't reproach us,   he'll bless us all instead." AOI

CXLIV

When Roland sees   this horde of infidels
Who all are darker   than is the blackest ink,
With nothing white   except their gleaming teeth,
He says aloud,   "There isn't any doubt,
Today we'll die—   I can believe it now.
Follow me, Frenchmen!   We'll give them one more charge!"
Oliver says,   "The devil take the last!"
The French attack;   their blows fall hard and fast.

CXLV

1940   And when the pagans   see how few Franks are left,
They take much pride   and comfort from the fact,
Telling each other,   "King Charles is in the wrong."
Then Marganice,   astride a sorrel horse,
Pricks with gold spurs   and gallops from behind
To land his spear   deep in Oliver's back.
The gleaming hauberk   shatters and splits away,
The spear goes through   and opens up his chest.
Says Marganice,   "You've taken a hard blow!
Charlemagne left you   to wait here for your doom.
1950   Let him not glory   in what he's done to Spain—
Your death alone   avenges all our slain."

CXLVI

Oliver feels   how close he is to death.
He raises high   Halteclere's bright burnished blade,
Strikes Marganice,   and splits his tall gold helm,
Its jewels and flowers   fall shattered to the ground;
He cleaves his head   right down into the teeth,
Wrenching the sword,   he hurls the body down.
Then says the count,   "Be damned, you Saracen!
Whatever Charles   may have lost here today,
At least I'm sure   no wife or lady friend   1960
Will hear you boasting,   safe in your lands again,
Of how you captured   silver or gold from me:
Your triumphs here   will not be on parade."
He summons then   Count Roland to his aid. AOI

CXLVII

Oliver knows   he has a fatal wound.
He'll never have his fill   of vengeance now.
In the melee   he fights on valiantly,
He cuts through spears,   the pagans' studded shields,
And feet and fists   and saddle-trees and spines.
Whoever watched him   cut pagans limb from limb,   1970
Bodies piled up   around him on the ground,
Would know that once   he'd seen a noble lord.
The count remembers   the war-cry of King Charles,
And loud and clear   his voice rings out, "Montjoie!"
He calls to Roland,   summons his friend and peer,
"My lord, companion,   come fight beside me now!
We'll part in sorrow   before the sun goes down." AOI

CXLVIII

Roland is there;   he sees Oliver's face,
The skin is ashen,   so pallid it looks grey,

1980 And from his wounds   bright blood is spurting out;
Its heavy drops   flow down him to the ground.
"O God!" says Roland,   "I don't know what to do.
Was such great valor   destined to be cut down!
My noble friend,   you'll have no peer on earth.
Alas, sweet France!   You are bereft today
Of your good vassals,   laid waste and brought to shame;
The Emperor Charles   will sorely feel the lack."
With these words Roland   faints on his horse's back. AOI

CXLIX

Here is Count Roland   unconscious on his horse;
1990 Oliver, wounded   and very close to death,
Has bled so much   that both his eyes are dimmed:
Now far or near   he can't see well enough
To give a name   to any man alive.
When he encounters   Count Roland in the field,
Oliver strikes him,   cleaving his golden helm
Brilliant with jewels—   the nose-piece cracks in two—
And yet the blade   does not touch face or head.
Roland's eyes open,   and looking at his friend,
Softly and gently   he asks him only this:
2000 "My lord, companion,   it's Roland—did you know?
I've always loved you;   did you intend that blow?
You gave no challenge   before you charged at me."
Oliver says,   "I recognize your voice,
But I can't see you—   God keep you in His sight!
I struck at you!   I pray you, pardon me."
Roland replies,   "I am not hurt at all;
I do forgive you,   here and in front of God."
When he had spoken,   each leaned down toward his friend.
So, with great love,   they parted in the end.

CL

2010 Oliver suffers   the agonies of death;
He feels his eyes   turn back into his head,

He cannot hear,   he cannot see at all.
Now he dismounts,   and kneeling on the ground,
Aloud he asks   forgiveness for his sins;
He clasps his hands,   and holds them toward the sky,
Praying that God   will grant him Paradise,
And give His blessing   to Charles and to sweet France,
And to Count Roland   above all other men.
Then his heart fails him,   his shining helmet bows.
All of his body   sinks down against the ground;   2020
The count is dead—   no longer did he stay.
Lord Roland weeps,   lamenting bitterly;
Many have grieved,   but no man more than he.

CLI

When Roland sees   that Oliver is dead,
Lying face downward   stretched out against the ground,
With tender words   he bids his friend farewell:
"Alas, companion!   Your valor ends in woe.
We were together   so many years and days;
You never wronged me,   and I kept faith with you.
Now you are dead,   I grieve to be alive."   2030
The marquis faints   just as he says these words,
Still on his horse,   whose name is Veillantif;
The fine gold stirrups   will keep him sitting straight,
So he won't fall   however he may sway.

CLII

Before Count Roland   recovers from his faint,

2013. The verb used to describe the position of Christians at prayer
is always *se culcher*, normally "to lie down." This seems, however, to
mean that they knelt. Here, for example, Oliver *se culchet*, but in line
2020 his whole body sinks to the ground.
2031. A *marchis* is the lord of a march, or border territory.
The only information Einhard gives about Roland is that he was
Count of the March of Brittany.

While he still sits   unconscious on his horse,
The battle brings   disaster to his men:
The Franks are dead—   he's lost them, every one
Save the archbishop   and Gautier de l'Hum
2040 Who from the mountains   has now returned at last.
He fought a battle   with Spanish Saracens.
His men are dead;   their enemies have won.
Down toward the valleys,   he flees now, all alone,
Searching for Roland,   calling to him for help:
"Ah, noble count!   Where are you, valiant lord?
When you were with me,   I never was afraid.
It's Gautier—   I conquered Maelgut!
Droon is my uncle,   his aged head is grey.
You used to love me,   because you knew me brave.
2050 My spear is broken,   my shield has been pierced through,
My hauberk's links   scattered and snapped apart,
Deep in my body   a pagan lance has thrust;
I'm dying now,   but they have bought me dear."
Roland wakes up   to hear his final words;
Turning his horse,   toward Gautier he spurs. AOI

CLIII

Count Roland, grieving   and filled with bitter rage,
Rides once again   through the thick of the fight.
Twenty Spaniards   he throws dead to the ground,
Gautier kills six,   Archbishop Turpin five.
2060 The pagans say,   "These men are monstrous fierce!
Take care, my lords,   don't let them get away.
If you aren't traitors,   we'll rush upon them now—
If you aren't cowards,   they won't escape alive!"
Then riding onward   with a great hue and cry,
They charge the Franks   once more from every side. AOI

2052. *Od lance sui feruz* supplied by Jenkins from V⁴. The line in the
Oxford manuscript is only half legible.
2055. Bédier indicates an omission after this *laisse*.

CLIV

There is Count Roland, a noble warrior,
Gautier de l'Hum, a worthy chevalier,
Archbishop Turpin, a veteran and brave:
None would be willing to fail the other two.
In the melee they strike the pagans down.   2070
A thousand Spaniards dismount to fight on foot,
While forty thousand stay on their horses' backs—
And even so they don't dare come too near.
They throw their lances, hurl their keen-bladed spears,
All sorts of weapons come flying at the Franks;
With the first blows, Count Gautier is killed,
Turpin of Reims soon finds his shield pierced through,
His helmet breaks— he's wounded in the head—
His chain-mail hauberk is cracked and splits apart,
Four pagan spears strike deep into his flesh,   2080
His war-horse, dying, carries him to the ground.
O God! What sorrow to see Turpin go down! AOI

CLV

Turpin of Reims, finding himself unhorsed,
With four deep wounds where spears thrust through his flesh,
Leaps up again, great fighter that he is,
Looks for Count Roland, and hastens to his side,
Saying just this: "I am not beaten yet!
No man of courage gives up while he's alive."
He draws Almace whose blade is burnished steel,
Strikes in the throng a thousand blows and more.   2090
Soon Charles will say that Turpin spared no foe:
They found four hundred around him in the field,
Some of them wounded, some of them thrust clean through,
And there were others who parted with their heads.
So says the *Geste,* and someone who was there:
Saint Giles for whom Our Lord works miracles

Left an account   in Laon's church in France;
Everyone knows this,   or nothing understands.

CLVI

Roland delivers   many a skillful blow,
2100   But now his body   is fevered, drenched with sweat,
His head is throbbing   under a dreadful pain,
His temples broken   from sounding his great horn.
Longing to know   if Charles is on his way,
Weakly, once more,   he blows the Oliphant.
King Charles stands still,   listening to that call;
"My lords," he says,   "now we have come to woe!
My nephew Roland   takes leave of us this day—
His horn's voice tells me   he won't be long alive.
Who wants to be there   had better speed his horse.
2110   Let every trumpet   the host commands resound!"
And sixty thousand   rang from the lofty peaks
Down through the valleys,   echoing loud and clear.
The pagans, listening,   think it no empty boast—
They say, "Here come   King Charles and all his host."   AOI

CLVII

The pagans say,   "Now Charles is coming back.
Those trumpet calls   rally the men of France;
We'll have great losses   if the Emperor comes,
And if Count Roland   lives to make war again,
We may as well   surrender all of Spain."
2120   About four hundred   assemble, helmeted,
The best who fought   among the Saracens;
With all their might   these men attack anew,
And then Count Roland   has work enough to do.   AOI

CLVIII

When Roland sees   the pagans closing in,
His heart grows stronger,   and prouder and more fierce.

He'll yield to none,   as long as he's alive.
Astride the horse   whose name is Veillantif,
He gallops toward them,   pricking with golden spurs;
Into the throng   he charges to attack.
Archbishop Turpin   is fighting at his side.   2130
The pagans say,   "Let's get away from here!
Those trumpet calls   mean that the Franks are near—
Their mighty king,   great Charles, will soon appear!"

CLIX

Count Roland's friendship   no coward ever knew,
Nor any man   false-hearted or too proud,
Nor any knight   who was not skilled at war.
To the archbishop   Roland addressed these words:
"I am on horseback,   my lord, and you're on foot;
For love of you,   here I shall take my stand—
We'll meet together   what good or evil comes,   2140
No mortal man   will make me leave your side.
We shall return   the Saracen attack.
What sword can equal   the blows of Durendal!
Turpin replies,   "Curse him whose arm grows slack!
We'll be avenged   when Charlemagne comes back."

CLX

The pagans say,   "Ours were unlucky stars!
Would that this evil day   had never dawned!
We've lost our peers,   our lords have all been slain,

2142-3. Jenkins rejects the two lines as given here, in favor of the V⁴
version which says, approximately: "Today, after this assault, the
pagans will know the names of Almace and Durendal." But Bédier,
I think quite rightly, finds no discourtesy to the Archbishop in the
line as it stands: the virtue is in the sword, not in Roland. And
Bédier calls attention to line 2350, where Roland speaks of "serving"
Durendal.

The valiant Charles   is coming back again.
2150 Now we can hear   the trumpets of his host,
The mighty clamor   when the Franks shout 'Montjoie!'
And this Count Roland   is hideously fierce—
He can't be conquered   by men of flesh and blood.
Let's cast our lances   and then leave him alone."
The Saracens   throw many javelins,
Lances and darts,   and feathered throwing spears.
Count Roland's shield   is broken and pierced through,
His hauberk's mail   is cracked and split apart,
And still his body   has not been touched at all.
2160 But Veillantif   has suffered thirty wounds;
Beneath Count Roland   he falls dead to the ground.
Then all the pagans   yield to their fear and flee;
And Roland stands,   dismounted, on the field. AOI

CLXI

The pagans flee,   furious and enraged,
Trying their best   to get away in Spain.
Count Roland lacks the means   to chase them now,
For he has lost   his war-horse Veillantif;
Against his will   he has to go on foot.
He went to give   Archbishop Turpin help,
2170 Unlaced his helmet,   removed it from his head,
And then took off   the hauberk of light mail;
The under-tunic   he cut into long strips
With which he stanched   the largest of his wounds.
Then lifting Turpin,   carried him in his arms
To soft green grass,   and gently laid him down.
In a low voice   Roland made this request:
"My noble lord,   I pray you, give me leave,
For our companions,   the men we held so dear,
Must not be left   abandoned now in death.
2180 I want to go   and seek out every one,
Carry them here,   and place them at your feet."

Said the archbishop, "I grant it willingly.
The field belongs, thank God, to you and me."

CLXII

Alone, Count Roland   walks through the battlefield,
Searching the valleys,   searching the mountain heights.
He found the bodies of Ivon and Ivoire,
And then he found   the Gascon Engélier.
Gerin he found,   and Gerier his friend,
He found Aton   and then Count Bérengier,
Proud Anseïs he found,   and then Samson,
Gérard the Old,   the Count of Roussillon.
He took these barons,   and carried every one   2190
Back to the place   where the archbishop was,
And then he put them   in ranks at Turpin's knees.
Seeing them, Turpin   cannot restrain his tears;
Raising his hand,   he blesses all the dead.
And then he says,   "You've come to grief, my lords!
Now in His glory,   may God receive your souls,
Among bright flowers   set you in Paradise!
It's my turn now;   death keeps me in such pain,
Never again   will I see Charlemagne."

CLXIII

Roland goes back   to search the field once more,   2200
And his companion   he finds there, Oliver.
Lifting him in his arms,   he holds him close,
Brings him to Turpin   as quickly as he can,
Beside the others   places him on a shield;
Turpin absolves him,   signing him with the cross,
And then they yield   to pity and to grief.
Count Roland says,   "Brother in arms, fair friend,
You were the son   of Renier, the duke
Who held the land   where Runers valley lies.

2185. The extra two lines were added by Bédier to his own
translation, although they are not found in the Oxford manuscript.
He felt that all the peers must have been listed.

2210   For breaking lances,   for shattering thick shields,
Bringing the proud   to terror and defeat,
For giving counsel,   defending what is right,
In all the world   there is no better knight."

CLXIV

When Roland sees   that all his peers are dead,
And Oliver   whom he so dearly loved,
He feels such sorrow   that he begins to weep;
Drained of all color,   his face turns ashen pale,
His grief is more   than any man could bear,
2220   He falls down, fainting   whether he will or no.
Says the archbishop,   "Baron, you've come to woe."

CLXV

When the archbishop   sees Roland on the ground,
He feels more sorrow   than he has ever known.
He reaches out   to grasp the Oliphant;
A swift stream waters   the plain at Roncevaux,
And there, for Roland,   he wants to fill the horn.
Taking short steps,   staggering, he sets out,
But in his weakness   he can't go very far—
He has no strength,   his wounds have bled too much;
2230   He doesn't travel   even a hundred feet
Before he falls—   his heart has given out.
Now death is trying   to put his soul to rout.

CLXVI

Meanwhile Count Roland   recovers from his faint,
He rises to his feet,   but with great pain.

2211 and 2213. These are nearly identical in the Oxford manuscript.
One is omitted here, as in Bédier's translation.
2225–6. The legend that Roland died of thirst must have its inadequate
source in this passage.

He looks around him,   he searches up and down;
Beyond the place   where his companions lie,
Prone on the grass,   he sees the noble lord,
Archbishop Turpin,   God's delegate on earth.
Count Roland hears him   confessing he has sinned,
With his clasped hands   held upward toward the sky,   2240
Praying that God   will give him Paradise.
Turpin is dead   who fought for Charlemagne.
With mighty blows,   with wise and holy words,
Against the pagans   he championed the Faith.
May God in heaven   bless him and grant him grace.

CLXVII

Roland sees Turpin   lying there on the ground,
Entrails protruding   from his enormous wounds;
Above his forehead   his brains are bubbling out.
On Turpin's chest,   between his collarbones,
Roland has crossed   the beautiful white hands.   2250
Now he laments   as it is done in France:
"O nobly born,   illustrious chevalier,
To heaven's glory   I now commend your soul;
Our Lord will never   be served more willingly.
Since the Apostles,   there has been none like you
To keep the Law,   and bring men to the Faith.
From pain and sorrow   may your free soul arise;
May you find open   the gates of Paradise!"

CLXVIII

Now Roland knows   that death is very near.
His ears give way,   he feels his brain gush out.   2260
He prays that God   will summon all his peers;
Then, for himself,   he prays to Gabriel.
Taking the horn,   to keep it from all shame,
With Durendal   clasped in his other hand,
He goes on, farther   than a good cross-bow shot,

West into Spain, crossing a fallow field.
Up on a hilltop, under two lofty trees,
Four marble blocks are standing on the grass.
But when he comes there, Count Roland faints once more,
2270 He falls down backward; now he is at death's door.

CLXIX

High are the hills and very high the trees,
The four great blocks of polished marble shine;
On the green grass the count is lying still.
A Saracen watches with steady eyes:
This man feigned death, hiding among the slain;
His face and body he had besmeared with blood.
Now he stands up and dashes forward fast—
He's handsome, strong and very valiant too,
But he won't live to profit from his pride;
2280 He falls on Roland, seizing him and his arms,
And says these words: "Charles' nephew lost the fight!
When I go home, his sword shall be my prize."
But as he pulls it, Roland comes back to life.

CLXX

Count Roland feels the pagan take his sword,
And opening his eyes, he says just this:
"You look to me like no one on our side!"
Raising the horn he'd wanted to keep safe,
He strikes the helmet shining with gold and jewels,
Shatters the steel, smashes the skull and bones;
2290 He puts both eyes out of the pagan's head,
And sends his body crashing against the ground.
And then he asks him, "How did you get so brave,
Dog, to attack me with or without just cause?
Whoever heard this would say you were insane!
But I have cracked the Oliphant's broad bell;
Its gold and crystals were shattered as it fell."

CLXXI

Count Roland feels   that he is going blind.
Now he stands upright,   using what strength remains;
All of the color   has vanished from his face.
In front of him   there is a dark grey stone.   2300
He strikes ten blows   in bitterness and grief;
The steel blade grates   but will not break or dent.
The count cries out,   "O Holy Mary, help!
O Durendal,   alas for your fair fame!
My life is over,   I'll care for you no more.
We've won such battles   together in the field,
So many lands   we've conquered, you and I,
For Charles to rule   whose beard is silver-grey.
No man must have you   who fights and runs away!
You have been long   in a good vassal's hands;   2310
You'll have no equal   in all of holy France."

CLXXII

Count Roland strikes   the bright carnelian stone;
The steel blade grates   but will not chip or break.
When Roland sees   he can't destroy his sword,
Then, to himself,   grieving, he speaks its praise:
"O Durendal,   how fair you are, and bright!
Against the sunlight   your keen steel gleams and flames!
Charles was that time   in Moriana's Vales
When by God's will   an angel from the sky
Said to bestow you   upon a chieftain count: 2320
The noble king   girded you at my side.
With you I won him   Anjou and Brittany,
Conquered Poitou   and after that all Maine,
With you I won him   that free land, Normandy,
Conquered Provence,   and then all Aquitaine,

2297. Jenkins considers this line impossible, and substitutes "Roland
feels that death is pressing him hard."

And Lombardy,   Romagna after that.
With you I won him   Bavaria, Flanders too,
And Burgundy,   the Polianis' lands;
Constantinople   paid homage to King Charles,
2330 In Saxony   he does as he desires.
With you I conquered   the Irish and the Scots,
And England too   the king holds as his own.
So many countries   we've won him, many lands
Ruled by King Charles   whose flowing beard is white.
For your sake now   I suffer grief and pain—
Better to die   than leave you here in Spain.
Almighty Father,   keep sweet France from that shame!"

CLXXIII

Count Roland strikes   against a dark grey stone;
More of it falls   than I can make you see.
2340 The steel blade grates   but will not crack or break;
Against the sky   it springs back up again.
Count Roland knows   he can't destroy his sword.
Then, to himself,   he quietly laments:
"O Durendal,   holy you are, and fair!
You have great relics   within your hilt of gold:
Saint Peter's tooth,   drops of Saint Basil's blood,
Hairs from the head   of my lord Saint Denis,
Part of a garment   that Holy Mary wore—
For any pagan   to hold you would be wrong;
2350 Only by Christians   can you be rightly served.
May you not fall   into a coward's hands!
Many wide lands   we've conquered, you and I,

2328. Jenkins prints "Honguerie," Burgundy having been a Frankish territory long before Charlemagne, and explains *trestote Poillánie* as indicated in my translation.

2331. Bédier leaves a blank where Mortier has *Vales Islonde* and Jenkins *Islande*. It seems likely that the latter is correct in translating "Ireland" rather than "Iceland."

For Charles to rule   whose flowing beard is white;
They have increased   his majesty and might."

CLXXIV

Count Roland feels   the very grip of death
Which from his head   is reaching for his heart.
He hurries then   to go beneath a pine;
In the green grass   he lies down on his face,
Placing beneath him   the sword and Oliphant;
He turns his head   to look toward pagan Spain.   2360
He does these things   in order to be sure
King Charles will say,   and with him all the Franks,
The noble count   conquered until he died.
He makes confession,   for all his sins laments,
Offers his glove   to God in penitence. AOI

CLXXV

Now Roland feels   his time has all run out.
He looks toward Spain   from high on a steep hill,
And with one hand   beating his breast, he says:
"God, I have sinned   against Thy holy name.
Forgive the sins,   the great ones and the less,   2370
That I committed   from my first hour of life
To this last day   when I have been struck down."
And now toward God   he raises his right glove;
A flight of angels   comes from the skies above. AOI

CLXXVI

And now Count Roland,   lying beneath a pine,
Has turned his face   to look toward pagan Spain;
And he begins   remembering these things:
The many lands   his valor won the king,
Sweet France, his home,   the men of his own line,
And Charlemagne   who raised him in his house—   2380

The memories   make him shed tears and sigh.
But not forgetting   how close he is to death,
He prays that God   forgive him all his sins:
"O my true Father,   O Thou who never lied,
Thou who delivered   Lazarus from the grave,
Who rescued Daniel   out of the lions' den,
Keep now my soul   from every peril safe,
Forgive the sins   that I have done in life."
Roland, in homage,   offers his glove to God.
2390 Saint Gabriel comes   and takes it from his hand.
His head sinks down   to rest upon his arm;
Hands clasped in prayer,   the count has met his end.
God sends from heaven   the angel Cherubin,
Holy Saint Michael   who saves us from the sea,
And with these two   the Angel Gabriel flies.
Count Roland's soul   they bring to Paradise.

CLXXVII

Roland is dead;   his soul rests now with God.
The Emperor Charles   rides into Roncevaux;
On every road,   on every mountain path,
2400 On every ell,   on every foot of land,
They find a body   of Frank or Saracen.
King Charles cries out,   "Fair nephew, where are you?
Where's the archbishop?   Where is Count Oliver?
Where is Count Gerin,   and Gerier his friend?
Oton—where is he,   and noble Bérengier,
Ivoire and Ivon,   those two I held so dear?
Tell me what happened   to Gascon Engelier,
Where are Duke Samson,   the valiant Anseïs,
And Old Gérard,   the Count of Roussillon?
2410 Where are the peers,   the twelve who stayed behind?"
What good is asking   when no one can reply?
"God!" says the king,   "Now have I cause to grieve,
For where was I   when fighting here began!"
He pulls his beard   in anguish and in pain;

The lords of France   are weeping bitter tears,
And twenty thousand   faint in their grief and fall.
Duke Naimon feels   great sorrow for them all.

CLXXVIII

There is not one   among those noble lords
Who can refrain   from shedding tears of grief:
It is their sons,   their brothers that they mourn,   2420
Their nephews, friends;   they weep for their liege lords.
Many among them   fall fainting to the ground.
Only Duke Naimon   can see what must be done;
He is the first   to tell the emperor:
"Look up ahead,   two leagues from where we stand,
See how the dust   is rising from the road—
There are the pagans,   and surely not a few.
Ride after them!   Let us avenge our grief!"
"O God," says Charles,   "they are already far—
Grant me this grace,   let me do what is right,   2430
For they have stolen   the flower of sweet France!"
The king commands   Oton and Geboïn,
Thibault of Reims,   and also Count Milon:
"Guard well this field,   the valleys and the heights,
Let all the dead   remain just as they are,
But keep them safe   from lions and wild beasts;
Let no one touch them,   no servant and no squire—
I say to you,   let no man touch these dead
Until God brings us   back to this field again."
They answer him   with reverence and love: 2440
"Right Emperor,   dear lord, as you command."
These four will keep   a thousand knights at hand. AOI

CLXXIX

The Emperor Charles   has all his trumpets sound.
The mighty lord   rides onward with his host;
They find the tracks   made by the Saracens,

And all together   follow them in pursuit.
When the king sees   that evening will come soon,
In a green meadow   he gets down from his horse,
Kneels on the ground   and prays almighty God
2450 To make the sun   stop moving through the sky,
Delay the night,   and let the day remain.
And then an angel,   who often spoke with him,
Came in great haste   to give him this command:
"Charles, speed you on!   The light won't fail you now.
God knows that you have lost   the flower of France.
You'll have your vengeance   on the vile Saracen!"
Already Charles   has mounted once again. AOI

CLXXX

For Charlemagne   God worked a miracle:
The sun stops moving,   and stands still in the sky.
2460 The pagans flee,   the Franks pursue them hard,
At Val-Tenebre   they overtake their foes;
Toward Saragossa   they chase them, sword in hand,
With mighty blows   cutting the pagans down,
Driving them off   the wide paths and the roads,
Until they find   the Ebro in their way.
Deep is the water,   and frightening and swift,
There are no boats,   no galleys, not a barge.
The Saracens   invoke their Tervagant;
They all jump in,   but nothing keeps them safe:
2470 The men in armor   weigh more than all the rest,
Some of them sink   straight down into the depths,
Others are carried   by the swift-running stream,
Those least in danger   still drink, and far too much;
All of them drown   in anguish and in fear.
The French cry, "Roland,   if only you were here!" AOI

CLXXXI

When Charlemagne   sees all the pagans dead,
Some slain in battle,   and many of them drowned,

Leaving great spoils   for all the Frankish knights,
The noble king,   dismounting from his horse,
Kneels on the ground,   and gives his thanks to God.   2480
When he gets up,   he sees the sun has set.
The emperor says,   "We'll have to make camp here.
It's too late now   to ride to Roncevaux—
All of our horses   are weary and worn out.
Take off their saddles   and let their bridles go;
Free in these meadows,   they'll cool off as they should."
The Franks reply,   "My lord, your words are good."   AOI

CLXXXII

The Emperor Charles   has had his camp set up.
The French dismount   there in the wilderness,
The horses' saddles   are taken off their backs,   2490
The golden bridles   are lifted from their heads,
They roam the meadows   where there is good fresh grass—
There are no other   provisions to be had.
Men who are weary   lie on the ground and sleep;
For on this night   there is no watch to keep.

CLXXXIII

Now in a meadow   the emperor lies down;
His mighty spear   he keeps close by his head,
For on this night   he wishes to stay armed.
He wears his hauberk   of saffron-burnished steel,
His helm is laced,   bright gems gleam in its gold;   2500
Still at his side,   Joyeuse, the peerless sword,
Which changes color   thirty times every day.
We all have heard   what happened to the lance
With which Our Lord   was wounded on the Cross:
Charles has the spearhead—   almighty God be thanked—
He had it mounted   into the golden hilt,
And for that honor,   that sign of heaven's love,
The name Joyeuse   was given to the sword.
Let the French barons   remember this each time

2510　They cry "Montjoie!"   in battle: let them know
　　　 That war cry means   they'll conquer any foe.

CLXXXIV

The night is clear,   the moon gleams in the sky.
King Charles lies down,   but for Count Roland grieves,
For Oliver   whose loss weighs on his heart,
For the twelve peers,   for all the men of France:
At Roncevaux   their bloodstained bodies lie.
He can't help weeping,   and bitterly laments,
Praying that God   have mercy on their souls.
The king is weary,   exhausted by his grief,
2520　He falls asleep—   he can't do any more.
In all the meadows   the Franks are sleeping too.
There's not one horse   left standing on its feet;
Those who want grass   eat just what they can reach.
A man does well   to learn what pain can teach.

CLXXXV

Charles goes to sleep   worn out by grief and toil.
Then God in heaven   sends Saint Gabriel down,
Commanding him   to guard the emperor.
The angel stays   close by his head all night,
And in two visions   lets him see what will come:
2530　Another foe   is marching on the king,
The dream shows clearly   the fighting will be grim.
The emperor sees   above him in the sky
Lightning and thunder,   and gusts of wind and hail,
Great are the tempests,   fearful and vast the storms,
The heavens gather   flickering fire and flames
Which all at once   fall down upon his men;
Ash-wood and apple,   their spear-shafts are ablaze,
Their shields are burning   down to the boss of gold,
The shafts snap off   from their keen-bladed spears,
2540　Their chain-mail crumples,   and their strong helms of steel.

With great dismay   Charles sees his knights attacked
By vicious beasts—   by leopards and by bears,
Serpents and vipers,   dragons and devils too,
And there are griffons,   thirty thousand and more,
All of them leaping,   charging against the Franks,
The Franks who cry,   "Charlemagne, help us now!"
And overwhelmed   by pity and by grief,
He starts out toward them,   but something interferes:
A mighty lion   springs at him from a wood,
Fearful to look at,   raging and proud and bold;   *2550*
He leaps, attacking   the person of the king.
Grappling each other   they wrestle violently:
But who will rise   a victor, who will fall?
The emperor sleeps   and does not wake at all.

CLXXXVI

Later that night   he had another dream:
He was in Aix;   on a dais he stood,
Holding a bear   bound tight with double chains.
Thirty more bears   came out of the Ardennes,
Each of them speaking   exactly like a man.
They said to Charles,   "Sire, give him back to us!   *2560*
It isn't right   for you to keep him here;
We cannot choose   but bring our kinsman help."
Out of the palace   there came a hunting dog
Who then attacked   the largest of the bears;
On the green grass   apart from all the rest,
While the king watched,   they fought a dreadful fight—
He could not see   which one of them would lose.
All this God's angel   revealed to Charlemagne.
The king slept on   until it was bright day.

2556. The word *perrun* means essentially a block of stone, whether it
is a mounting block, a place where the king sits on formal occasions,
or one of the stones on which Roland tries to break Durendal.

CLXXXVII

2570 To Saragossa   the pagan king has fled.
There he dismounts   beneath an olive tree,
Gives up his sword,   his hauberk and his helm;
On the green grass   the king lies down in shame.
Marsile's right hand   was cut completely off,
And he is fainting   from loss of blood and pain.
In front of him,   his wife Queen Bramimonde,
Weeping for grief,   cries out a loud lament.
The queen has with her   some twenty thousand men,
All of them cursing   Charlemagne and sweet France.
2580 Now they attack   Apollo in his crypt,
Reviling him,   disfiguring his form:
"Why, evil god,   have you brought us to shame?
Why have you suffered   the downfall of our king?
For faithful service   you give a poor reward!"
Then they take off   his scepter and his crown,
And to a column   they tie him by the hands;
They knock him down,   stamping him with their feet,
And with great clubs   they smash him into bits.
They take the ruby   away from Tervagant,
2590 And then Mohammed   they thrust into a ditch
Where he'll be trampled   and gnawed by dogs and pigs.

CLXXXVIII

When King Marsile   recovers from his faint,
They carry him   into his vaulted room
Where bright designs   are painted on the walls.
And Bramimonde,   the queen, comes weeping there,
Tearing her hair,   deploring her sad fate;
In bitter grief   she cries these words aloud:
"O Saragossa,   how you have been despoiled!
You've lost that king   who was your noble lord!
2600 We are betrayed,   abandoned by our gods,

Those gods who failed him   this morning on the field.
The great emir   will do a craven thing
Unless he comes   and fights these valiant Franks
Too proud to care   whether they live or die.
As for King Charles   whose flowing beard is white—
He has great valor;   he's arrogant and bold,
If there's a battle   he's sure to stand his ground.
Alas! that no one   can bring this hero down!"

CLXXXIX

The Emperor Charles   by force of arms has stayed
Seven long years   at war in pagan Spain.   2610
He's taken castles   and conquered many towns.
The king, Marsile,   has tried hard to resist.
In the first year   he sent a message, sealed,
To Baligant,   Emir of Babylon.
Ancient of days   was this most noble lord—
He had outlived   Virgil and Homer both:
Let him bring help   to Saragossa's king,
Or else Marsile   will cast away his gods,
Give up the idols   to which he always prayed,
And turn instead   to holy Christian law,   2620
Ask Charlemagne   to set the terms for peace.
But Baligant,   far off, has long delayed;
From forty kingdoms   he has his vassals come,
His great swift ships   prepare to cross the sea,
Galleys and barges   and sailing craft for war.
There is a harbor   near Alexandria

2609. This is the beginning of the Baligant episode. It is also the
second time that the poet returns to the beginning of his poem, as
in 703.
2614. I have translated this debated line according to Bédier's interpretation. It could also mean that Baligant was born at the time of Virgil
and Homer—very long ago—and is still alive. The intention, in either
case, would be to emphasize the emir's great age, which is as fabulous
as Charlemagne's.

Where Baligant makes ready all his fleet;
In early summer, during the month of May
His pagan hosts at last get under way.

CXC

2630 Great is the might of those vile infidels;
They go by sail, they use their oars and steer.
Up on the masts and set in the high prows
Are many lanterns and ruby-colored stones
Which from above send forth such beams of light
That all night long the sea is beautiful.
When they come close, ready to land in Spain,
Their brightness passing lights up the countryside,
And King Marsile soon learns they have arrived. AOI

CXCI

The pagan hosts, impatient of delay,
2640 Turn from the sea and take the river road,
Passing Marbrise, leaving Marbrose behind,
Along the Ebro speeds their enormous fleet.
The ships are sparkling with lanterns and red stones
Which through the darkness illuminate their way.
At Saragossa they anchor the next day. AOI

CXCII

Fair is the morning, the sun shines clear and bright.
Now from his ship the emir disembarks,
Espanaliz comes forward on his right;
Seventeen kings are following their lord,
2650 And I can't tell you how many dukes and counts.
Under a laurel which in a meadow stands,
A white silk carpet is spread on the green grass;

2634. Jewels, particularly "carbuncles," were commonly considered sources
of illumination.

An ivory throne   is set on it, and there
The emir sits,   the pagan Baligant,
With all the others   remaining on their feet.
Their overlord   was the first one to speak:
"Listen to me,   you noble, valiant knights!
King Charlemagne,   Emperor of the Franks,
Has not the right to eat,   if I say no.
He has waged war   through all my lands in Spain;   2660
Now, in return,   I'll seek him in sweet France—
I won't give up   while life is left in me,
Until he's dead,   or bows to his defeat."
Baligant strikes   his right glove on his knee.

CXCIII

Once he has said it,   nothing will change his mind—
All the world's gold   could not dissuade him now—
He'll go to Aix   where Charlemagne holds court;
Then all his vassals   praise him and so advise.
Baligant summons   two of his chevaliers,
One, Clarifan,   the other Clarien: 2670
"You are the sons   of King Maltraïen
Who served me often   as my ambassador.
It is my will   that you go to Marsile
In Saragossa;   tell him that I have come
To bring him help   against the men of France:
Given the chance,   I'll wage a mighty war.
Take with you, folded,   this gold-embroidered glove;
Let the king set   this pledge on his right hand,
And give Marsile   this envoy's staff of gold.
Say I expect   his homage for his fief.   2680
I'll go to France   and challenge Charlemagne,

2668. Some commentators have noted a contrast here between the auto-
cratic Baligant and Charlemagne's more democratic tendencies. It is
certainly true that Charlemagne asks for and accepts the advice of
his council, providing they suggest nothing outrageous (262), and that
the poet calls our attention to this most emphatically (161–162).

And he will beg   for mercy at my feet,
He will renounce   his Christianity,
Or else I'll take   the crown right off his head!"
The pagans say,   "He'll be your man or dead."

CXCIV

Baligant says,   "You barons, mount and ride!
One take the staff,   the other take the glove."
And they reply,   "Dear lord, as you command."
They gallop on,   and come into the town;
2690 There are ten gates,   four bridges that they cross,
They pass through streets   where all the townsfolk live,
And as they climb   up to the highest place
They hear an uproar   inside the palace walls:
There are great numbers   of pagan Saracens
Weeping and shouting   and crying out in pain,
Mourning the gods,   Mohammed, Tervagant,
Apollo too,   which they possess no more.
They all are saying,   "What will become of us?
We are struck down   and utterly destroyed,
2700 For we have lost   our rightful king, Marsile:
Yesterday Roland   cut his right hand clean off;
Nor shall we see   blond Jurfaleu again.
Now all of Spain   surrenders to that count!"
The messengers   from Baligant dismount.

CXCV

They leave their horses   beneath an olive tree;
Two Saracens   have taken up the reins.

2691. Burgeis—the oldest known occurrence of this word (Jenkins).
2696. Jenkins' interpretation, "They curse the gods . . . from whom
they had no help," is attractive, and his reference to line 1172 where
the same expression, *n'aveir mie de,* is used in this way is quite
convincing. On the other hand, the pagans *pleignent* the gods, and this
word is generally used to mean "mourn for."

The envoys, holding   each other by the cloak,
Enter the palace,   go up long flights of stairs,
And when they reach   the king's high-vaulted room,
They greet him in good faith   with clumsy words: *2710*
"We pray Mohammed   who has us in his care,
Our lord Apollo   and mighty Tervagant,
To save the king   and to protect the queen!"
Bramimonde says,   "Who speaks that way is mad!
Those gods of ours   are traitors one and all.
At Roncevaux   they worked such miracles
That our brave knights   were slaughtered by the Franks;
As for my husband,   they failed him in the fight,
And his right hand   was cut completely off—
That mighty lord   Count Roland did the deed.   *2720*
This land of Spain   will all belong to Charles!
Wretched, abandoned,   what is my destiny?
If you were kind,   you'd make an end to me!" AOI

CXCVI

Says Clarien,   "Lady, don't talk so much!
We are the envoys   of pagan Baligant.
He guarantees   protection for Marsile—
In pledge of that   he sends this staff and glove.
Out on the Ebro   we have four thousand boats,
Sailing ships, barges,   swift-running galleys too,
And other vessels,   more than a man could count.   *2730*
The great emir   is powerful and rich;
He will go hunting   for Charlemagne in France,
And make him choose: the pagan faith or death."
Bramimonde says,   "No need to go so far!
It's where you are right now   you'll find the Franks!
For seven years   they've overrun this land.
A fighting lord   is Charles their emperor—
He'd rather die   than run from any field;
No king on earth   but seems to him a child.
Charles has no fear   of any man alive!"   *2740*

CXCVII

"Now that's enough!"   Marsile says to the queen,
And to the envoys: "Address yourselves to me.
My lords, you see   that I am close to death;
I have no son,   no daughter, and no heir—
The one I had   was killed just yesterday.
Say to my lord   that I would see him here.
Cairo's emir   can make good claim to Spain;
He'll have my kingdom,   if that is his desire—
But let him guard it well   against the Franks!
2750   I'll give him counsel   regarding Charlemagne:
He'll hold him captive   just one month from today.
Here are the keys   to Saragossa's walls;
Tell the emir   to trust me and remain."
"My lord," they answer,   "your words are true and plain."

                                                    AOI

CXCVIII

Marsile says this: "The Emperor of France
Killed all my men,   my kingdom he laid waste,
My towns and cities   he captured and destroyed.
He lay last night   close to the Ebro's banks;
I know the distance—   not more than seven leagues.
2760   Tell the emir   to lead his army there.
Give him my message: the time is ripe for war."
Keys of the city   he sends to Baligant;
Both messengers   bow low to King Marsile
And go their way   when they have taken leave.

CXCIX

Now the two envoys   have mounted once again;
They leave the city   as fast as they can go,

With great excitement   they rush to their emir,
Give him the keys   to Saragossa's walls.
Baligant says, "And what have you found out?
Where is Marsile   whom I had summoned here?"   2770
Clarien says,   "He's wounded unto death.
King Charles was crossing   the mountains yesterday,
For he intended   to go back to sweet France;
His noblest barons   were left to guard the pass:
The king's own nephew,   Count Roland, stayed behind,
Oliver too—   all the twelve peers of France,
And twenty thousand   were with them, men at arms.
They were attacked   by the brave king Marsile;
When he and Roland   met on the battlefield,
Durendal struck him   so terrible a blow   2780
That his right hand   was severed from his arm;
His son was killed,   whom he so dearly loved,
And all the barons   who fought there at his side.
He fled the battle—   he could not stand his ground—
And Charlemagne   pursued him on the field.
King Marsile swears   that if you save him now
You'll take possession   of all the lands of Spain."
And Baligant   listens to news so bad
With mournful thoughts   that nearly drive him mad. AOI

CC

"My lord emir,"   continues Clarien,   2790
"Just yesterday   they fought at Roncevaux.
Roland was killed,   and so was Oliver,
All the twelve peers   whom Charlemagne held dear,
And twenty thousand,   the warriors of France.
There King Marsile   had his right hand cut off,
The Emperor Charles   pursued him from the field;
In all this kingdom   no chevalier is left—

2767. "Yesterday" should perhaps not be taken literally. Similarly,
line 2791.

They all were slain, or in the Ebro drowned.
Close to the river the French have made their camp:
2800 From where we stand, the distance is so short
That, if you wish it, they'll have a hard road home."
Now Baligant looks fierce and proud again;
Great is the joy he feels within his heart.
All of a sudden he leaps up to his feet
Shouting aloud, "My barons, get you gone!
Out of the boats! Now is the time to ride!
If we don't let old Charlemagne escape,
For King Marsile prompt payment I'll demand,
And send him back a head for his right hand."

CCI

2810 The Arab pagans, leaving their boats behind,
With all speed mount their horses and their mules,
And ride away— that's what they're told to do.
The great emir who roused their will to war
Summons Gemalfin, a favorite of his:
"While I am gone, my hosts are in your care."
He mounts his dark brown charger, and rides away;
Four noble dukes follow him close behind.
At Saragossa he rides into the town,
And then draws rein beside a marble block;
2820 Four counts are there to hold the stirrups taut
While he dismounts. He climbs the palace stairs,
And Bramimonde comes running up to him,
Crying aloud, "Alas that I was born!
I've lost my husband; Sire, I am left to shame."
He lifts her up, as she falls at his feet;
Now they have gone to King Marsile's retreat.

CCII

When King Marsile sees Baligant come in,

He quickly summons two Spanish Saracens:
"Give me your help— I want to sit up straight."
In his left hand he holds one of his gloves.   2830
Then says Marsile, "My lord and king, emir,
I now hand over all of my lands to you,
And Saragossa with all it holds in fief.
I've brought myself to ruin, my people too."
The emir answers, "I grieve to learn of this,
And there's no time for us to talk at length—
Charles isn't waiting, I know, to fight with me,
But just the same I do accept your glove."
And so, in sorrow, weeping, he turns away. AOI
He leaves the palace, down the long flights of stairs,   2840
Gets on his horse and spurs back to his men.
He gallops hard until he leads them all;
Often he shouts to urge them to the fray,
"Pagans, come on! Don't let them get away!" AOI

CCIII

Early next morning when the bright dawn appears,
The Emperor Charles awakens from his sleep.
Saint Gabriel, whom God sent to keep watch,
Blesses the king, making his holy sign.
Charlemagne rises; he takes his armor off,
Throughout the hosts men put their weapons down,   2850
They mount their horses, and ride with utmost speed
Down the long paths, along the broad straight road;
They will have cause for wonder and great woe,
There where the battle was fought at Roncevaux. AOI

2837–38. Jenkins interprets this to mean that the official defender of the
fief is still Marsile, and Baligant courteously regrets taking the glove
which is the symbol of his authority. Line 2837 could mean simply
that Baligant must hurry while Charles is still close at hand, but this
would make it hard to explain "just the same" in the following line.
Obviously the ceremony did not take very long.

CCIV

King Charlemagne   returns to Roncevaux.
He sees the dead;   his eyes are filled with tears.
He tells the Franks,   "My lords, walk slowly on;
I'll go before you   into the battlefield—
I know I'll find   my nephew's body there.
2860 One time at Aix   during a solemn feast,
My valiant knights   were making boastful vows
To fight great battles   and do heroic deeds.
I heard my nephew   say he could promise this:
If he must die   fighting in some strange land,
We'd find his body   beyond his men and peers,
His head still turned   to face the enemy;
He'd end his life   in valor, conquering."
A greater distance   than flies a stick well thrown,
He goes ahead,   then climbs a hill alone.

CCV

2870 The emperor, seeking   the place where Roland fell,
Crosses a meadow   covered with plants whose flowers
Are all stained crimson   with the life-blood of France.
He feels such sorrow   he cannot help but weep.
And now he finds,   close to the two great trees,
Three blocks of stone   where Durendal cut deep;
On the green grass   he sees his nephew, dead.
It is no wonder   he's overwhelmed with woe.
The king dismounts   and runs across the field.
He takes Count Roland   and holds him in his arms,
2880 Falls with him, fainting,   his grief so racks his heart.

CCVI

The Emperor Charles   recovers from his faint;
Naimon the Duke,   with him Count Acelin,

Geoffroy of Anjou,   his brother called Thierry,
Go to the king,   lean him against a pine.
And Charles looks down;   he sees his nephew dead.
With words of praise,   softly, he says farewell:
"Roland, my friend,   may God forgive your sins!
Never on earth   was there a knight like you
To fight great battles   in triumph to the end.
From this time forth   my honor will decline."   2890
He cannot help it: he faints a second time. AOI

CCVII

Again the king   recovers from his faint;
Four of his barons   support him by his hands;
King Charles looks down   at Roland lying dead,
So handsome still,   but he is ashen pale,
His eyes turned upward,   dark shadows in their place.
Then Charlemagne   with love and faith laments:
"Roland, my friend,   may your soul rest in flowers
In Paradise,   among the holy saints!
The fault is mine   that you found death in Spain!   2900
No day will dawn   but that I'll grieve for you.
This is the end   of all my strength and pride!
Who will uphold   Charlemagne's honor now?
In all the world   there's no friend left to me;
I have no kinsmen   so gallant and so brave."
With both his hands   he tears his silver hair.
The sight so moves   a hundred thousand Franks
There is not one   dry-eyed in all their ranks. AOI

CCVIII

"Roland, my friend,   I'm going home to France;
There in Laon   when I hold court once more,   2910

2899. That is, "the glorious ones."
2900. "What a bad lord you followed to Spain!" Bédier questions the
meaning of this, but at least Charlemagne's self-reproach is apparent.

Strangers will come from kingdoms all around,
And they will ask me, 'Where is the chieftain count?'
And I will tell them that Roland died in Spain.
In bitter sorrow my kingdom I will keep;
No day will dawn when I don't mourn and weep."

CCIX

"Roland, my friend, valiant and young and fair,
Aix la Chapelle will see my court again,
And men will come asking to hear the news.
I'll give them tidings cruel and full of woe:
2920 'Dead is my nephew who won me such great lands.'
Against my rule the Saxons will rebel,
Hungarians, Bulgars, so many pagan tribes,
Romans, Apulians, the men of Sicily,
And Africans, and men of Califerne;
A time of toil and hardship will begin—
Who will command my hosts to victory,
Since he is dead who led us in the field?
Alas, sweet France! How empty you will be!
I feel such sorrow I wish I were no more."
2930 King Charlemagne pulls at his silver beard,
He tears his hair, twisting it with both hands.
A hundred thousand fall fainting where they stand.

CCX

"Roland, my friend, may God forgive your sins!
Now may your soul rejoice in Paradise!
Whoever killed you struck down the pride of France.
I feel such sorrow I have no wish to live,
Mourning those men who died here serving me.
I pray that God, the blessed Mary's son,

2935. Perhaps the poet meant to remind his audience that Roland, in
fact, killed himself. He died not of battle wounds but of the injury
he suffered in the tremendous effort of blowing the Oliphant.

Will let me die before I come to Cize,
That soul and body part company today.   *2940*
Among their souls mine too would have its place,
My flesh and theirs be buried side by side."
He pulls his beard, and from his eyes tears flow.
Duke Naimon says, "Now Charles feels bitter woe." AOI

CCXI

"Lord emperor," Geoffroy of Anjou says,
"Control yourself; do not give way to grief.
Have the field searched for bodies of our men
Killed in the battle by Spanish Saracens,
And to one grave command that they be borne."
The king replies, "So be it; sound your horn!" AOI   *2950*

CCXII

Geoffroy of Anjou has blown a trumpet call;
The French dismount at Charlemagne's command
To seek their friends dead on the battlefield,
And put their bodies into a common grave.
The many bishops and abbots who are there,
The monks and canons and all the tonsured priests
Absolve the dead and sign them with the cross.
They kindle incense, light aromatic myrrh:
From swinging censers arise sweet clouds of smoke.
They closed the grave with all the rites they knew,   *2960*
And turned away— what else was there to do? AOI

CCXIII

Then Charles has Roland made ready for the grave,
And Oliver, Archbishop Turpin too,
Their chests cut open while he himself looks on,
The three men's hearts withdrawn and wrapped in silk,
And in a coffin of pure white marble placed.

When that is done, the bodies of the lords
Are taken up and washed with spice and wine;
Around each baron they place a deerskin shroud.
2970 Charlemagne orders Thibault and Geboin,
Milon the count and the marquis Oton
To lead the carts in which they were conveyed,
All covered over with palls of silk brocade. AOI

CCXIV

The Emperor Charles is anxious to depart,
But pagan outposts rise up along his way.
Then from the closest, two messengers arrive;
For Baligant, they summon Charles to war:
"This is no time, proud king, to go away!
The great emir is riding on your heels
2980 With all the hosts he led across the sea.
We'll know today what courage you command!" AOI
At that King Charles, his hand upon his beard,
Thinks once again of all that he has lost.
With fiery pride he gazes at his men,
Then in a voice mighty and clear he cries,
"Barons of France, take up your arms and ride!" AOI

CCXV

King Charles is first to arm himself for war.
Wasting no time, he puts his hauberk on,
Laces his helm; Joyeuse hangs at his side,
2990 The blade whose brilliance outshines the very sun.
Around his neck the king has placed his shield;
He brandishes the steel point of his spear,
And now he mounts his good horse Tencendur,
Won in a battle close to Marsone's ford
Where Charles' spear felled Malpalin de Nerbone.
He frees the reins, and spurring quick and hard,

Before the host   he gallops on parade;   AOI
God and Saint Peter   he summons to his aid.

CCXVI

All through the field   the men of France dismount;
A hundred thousand   put on their gear for war.   *3000*
They have equipment   such as their hearts desire,
Beautiful weapons   and horses bred for speed;
Mounted, they look   as if they'd fight with skill,
Given a chance,   they'll prove it on the field.
Their battle flags   hang down to touch their helms.
Charlemagne sees   how splendid they appear,
And this he tells   Jozeran of Provence,
Naimon the Duke,   Antelme de Mayence:
"In such brave knights   a man can place his trust;
Only a fool,   with such a host, despairs.   *3010*
And if these Arabs   don't change their minds and flee,
The price they'll pay   for Roland won't be low."
Duke Naimon answers,   "God grant that it be so."   AOI

CCXVII

Charlemagne summons   Rabel and Guinemant,
And says to them,   "My lords, hear my command:
In Roland's place   and Oliver's you'll ride;
One bear the sword,   and one the Oliphant.
You two shall be   the leaders of my host,
And you'll be followed   by fifteen thousand Franks,
Young nobles all,   the bravest in the land.   *3020*
And after these,   as many men again
Will be commanded   by Geboin and Lodrant."
Naimon the Duke,   with him Count Jozeran,
Set these divisions   in order for the field.
If there's a battle   they won't be quick to yield.   AOI

3003. So Jenkins' glossary interprets *unt grant science.*

CCXVIII

The first divisions   are filled up by the French,
And after these   they organize a third.
The vassals in it   are all Bavarians,
Their forces number   some twenty thousand knights.
3030 These men in battle   will never break their line;
In all the world   King Charles holds none so dear
Except the French   who won him all his realm.
That valiant fighter,   Count Ogier the Dane,
Leads this division   proud of its famous name.   AOI

CCXIX

The Emperor Charles   has three divisions now;
Naimon the Duke   establishes a fourth
Made up of barons,   loyal and very brave,
The Alemans   who come from Germany.
The others count them   as twenty thousand men.
3040 They're well equipped   with horses and with arms;
Not even death   can make them quit the field.
These soldiers Herman,   the Duke of Trace, will lead;
He'd rather die   than do a coward's deed.   AOI

CCXX

And then Duke Naimon,   with him Count Jozeran,
Formed a division   of men from Normandy,
Some twenty thousand,   according to the Franks.
They have fine weapons,   swift-running horses too;
Not even death   will ever make them yield.
No better fighters   exist in all the world;
3050 Richard the Old   will lead them in the fray—
Many a pagan   his sharpened spear will slay.   AOI

3041. For the mysterious "Thrace," Jenkins suggests Suabia or Alsace.

CCXXI

The sixth division,   made up of Breton knights,
Has thirty thousand   among its chevaliers,
A noble sight   as they ride forth to war
With painted lances   and waving battle-flags.
A man called Eudon   is leader of these men.
This is the order   he gives Count Nevelon,
Thibault of Reims,   and the marquis Oton:
"You'll take the lead;   this honor you have won."

CCXXII

The Emperor Charles   has six divisions now;   3060
Duke Naimon starts   to make a seventh one:
Men of Poitou,   and lords of the Auvergne.
Some forty thousand   number these chevaliers,
All with good horses   and the best kind of arms.
These, in a valley   protected by a hill,
Are grouped apart;   Charles blessed them with his hand.
Jozeran, Godselme   will have them to command.

CCXXIII

The eighth division   Duke Naimon organized,
Made up of Flemings   and knights from Friedland too,
Has forty thousand   among its ranks, and more.   3070
These are not likely   to run away from war.
Thus spoke the king: "They'll serve me very well."
Two leaders, Rembalt   and Hamon de Galice,
Will lead these troops   to brave and knightly feats.

CCXXIV

After that, Naimon,   with him Count Jozeran,
Made up another   brigade of valiant men,

Some from Lorraine,   others from Burgundy;
They say it numbered   some fifty thousand knights.
Their helms are laced,   they have their hauberks on,
3080   Their spears are heavy   with shafts cut very short.
If any Arabs   venture to come their way,
They'll strike them down   until the war is won;
They follow Thierry,   the duke of the Argonne. AOI

CCXXV

The tenth division   has none but lords of France,
The best of chieftains,   a hundred thousand strong.
Powerful looking,   their bearing fierce and proud;
Their heads and beards   are glistening with white.
They wear mail hauberks   and byrnies double thick;
They gird on swords   which come from France or Spain,
3090   Their shields are bright   with colors and designs.
And now they mount,   all asking for the fight,
"Montjoie!" they cry;   with them rides Charlemagne.
Geoffroy of Anjou   carries the Oriflamme—
It was Saint Peter's,   and then was called Romaine;
Among the Franks   Montjoie has been its name.

CCXXVI

The Emperor Charles   stops and gets off his horse,
On the green grass   he kneels, his head bent low,
And turns his face   to meet the rising sun.
He calls on God,   and prays most earnestly:
3100   "Father in Heaven,   protect me on this day
As Thou in truth   didst rescue Jonah once
When he was captured   and held inside a whale,
As thou didst spare   the King of Nineveh,
And rescued Daniel   from fearful suffering
When he was thrown   inside the lion's den;
And those three children   set in the midst of flames—

3090. That is, identifying insignia.
3094. That is, Charlemagne's banner.

So may Thy love   be close to me today!
And in Thy mercy   be gracious to my plea
That Roland's vengeance   may be allowed to me."
His prayer finished,   King Charles stands up again;   3110
The sign of power   he makes upon his brow.
And then the king   mounts his swift-running horse,
His stirrup held   by Naimon, Jozeran;
He takes his shield   and his sharp-pointed spear.
A handsome man,   the emperor, and strong,
His face is calm,   his bearing very proud;
He rides to battle,   as one with his great horse.
The clear-voiced trumpets   ring out from every side—
Above the others   resounds Count Roland's horn;
Then all the Frenchmen   remember him and mourn.   3120

CCXXVII

In all his splendor   the emperor rides on.
Outside his hauberk   he shows his long white beard;
For love of him,   the others do the same:
So were distinguished   his hundred thousand Franks.
They cross those mountains   crested with rocky peaks,
Those deep-set valleys,   those terrible ravines,
Out of the pass,   through the wastelands again—
Once more for Spain   the Franks have set their course.
On a plateau   they make camp for the night.
The pagan outposts   return to Baligant,   3130
And now a Syrian   tells what they have to say:
"Our eyes have seen   the arrogant King Charles.
His men are proud;   nothing will make them flee.
Take up your arms!   The battle is at hand!"
Says Baligant,   "Brave news, and I rejoice.
Summon my pagans   by the shrill trumpet's voice!"

CCXXVIII

Throughout the host   now beat the pagan drums,

Clarion horns and clear-voiced trumpets sound.
The men dismount to arm themselves for war.
3140 The great emir, impatient of delay,
Puts on a byrnie of saffron-burnished mail,
Laces his helmet shining with gold and jewels;
At his left side Baligant girds his sword
Which in his pride he honored with a name:
He had been told of Charlemagne's Joyeuse,
And so he called his own sword Précieuse;
He chose that name to be his war-cry too.
He has it shouted by all his chevaliers.
Around his neck he places his broad shield,
3150 Its boss is gold with crystals all around,
The strap embroidered with circles on brocade;
The spear he holds has Evil for its name,
Its mighty shaft looks like a rafter beam;
The tip itself would overload a mule.
Now Baligant has mounted his war-horse,
The stirrup held by Marcules d'Oltremer.
To carry him a horse needs a broad back;
The emir's hips are slender, his chest is wide
With well-sprung ribs, and beautifully shaped;
3160 He has broad shoulders, good color in his face,
A proud expression; his head of curling hair
Is just as white as any summer flower.
As for his courage, he's proved it many times.
God! What a hero if he had been baptized!
He spurs his horse— the bright red blood spurts out—
And gallops forward, leaping a mighty ditch:
Some fifty feet it measures at the least.
The pagans cry, "This lord will lose no lands!
If any Frenchman should dare to joust with him,
3170 He'll have no choice but swiftly will be slain;
Charles is a fool for choosing to remain!" AOI

3152. That is, "Maltet."

CCXXIX

This Baligant   looks like a noble lord.
His shining beard   is white as any flower.
He has great wisdom   concerning pagan law,
And once in battle   he's arrogant and fierce.
He has a son,   Malpramis, a fine knight,
Powerful, tall,   resembling his forebears.
"Sire, let's ride on!"   he says to Baligant,
"I'll be surprised   if we find Charlemagne."
His father answers,   "He's valiant; he'll be there.   *3180*
The chronicles   give him the highest praise.
But since Count Roland,   his nephew, is no more,
He has no power   to challenge us in war."   AOI

CCXXX

"Fair son, Malpramis,"   the emir said to him,
"The other day   that noble knight was slain,
Oliver too,   so valiant and so wise,
All the twelve peers   King Charles once held so dear,
And twenty thousand   who came with them from France.
All of the others   I count not worth a glove.
The Emperor Charles   is coming back again;   *3190*
My messenger,   the Syrian, reports
That ten divisions   are under his command.
A valiant lord   now sounds the Oliphant,
From his companion   a trumpet call comes back:

3179. In Jenkins' interpretation Malpramis asks if he will feel wonder
if they meet Charles, to which Baligant replies that he will, because
Charlemagne is a hero, and in many celebrated families (*gestes*) there
are great possessions (*granz honors*) which come from him. None of
this seems to me convincing, although between the unlikely arrogance
of Bédier's text and the improbable diffidence of Jenkins' version, it is
rather hard to choose. Perhaps it would be more natural to praise
Charles's valor here than his success as a land-bestowing leader.
3193–4. That is, Rabel and Guinemant.

These two are riding   as leaders of the host,
And they are followed   by fifteen thousand Franks
Charles calls his children: brave warriors, and young.
The next division   is just as large again.
These men will fight   with all the pride they show."
3200   Malpramis says,   "Then let me have first blow."   AOI

CCXXXI

"Fair son, Malpramis,"   says Baligant to him,
"You shall be granted   the boon that you have asked;
Against the Franks,   and soon, you'll strike your blow.
You shall have with you   Torleu, the Persian king,
And Dapamort,   the ruler of the Wilzes.
If you succeed   in putting down their pride,
You'll call your own   that portion of my land
From Cheriant   as far as Val-Marchis."
Malpramis answers,   "My lord, you have my thanks."
3210   Then coming forward,   the prince receives that gift,
The realm that once   belonged to King Florit;
The land is given   in such an evil hour
He'll never see it,   or hold it in his power.

CCXXXII

The great emir   goes riding through his hosts,
With tall Malpramis   following close behind.
Then the two kings,   Torleu and Dapamort,
Thirty divisions   establish with all speed;
Great is the number   of knights assembled there,
With fifty thousand   forming the least brigade.
3220   The first division   has men of Butentrot,
And in the second   big-headed men from Misnes—
They have stiff hairs   growing along their spines
Just like the bristles   along the backs of pigs.   AOI
The third is formed   of Nubians and Blos,
The fourth division   contains the Bruns and Slavs,

And in the fifth   they place Sorbres and Sors;
Then in the sixth   Armenians and Moors,
And in the seventh   the men from Jerico;
The eighth are blacks,   the ninth composed of Gros,
The tenth all come   from Balide la Forte—   3230
There is a tribe   which never loved the good!   AOI
Baligant vows   by what he holds most high,
Mohammed's body   and holy miracles:
"Now like a madman   comes riding Charles of France.
There'll be a battle,   unless he flees instead.
He'll wear no longer   a gold crown on his head!"

CCXXXIII

Ten more divisions   are made up after these:
The first contains   the ugly Canaanites
Who from Val-Foït   have made their way across;
The second, Turks;   Persians are in the third;   3240
The fourth contains   the savage Petchenegs,
The fifth has men   from Solteras, Avers;
The sixth has men   from Ormaleus, Eugiez,
And in the seventh   are Samuel's Bulgars;
The eighth from Bruise,   the ninth comes from Clavers,
The tenth from Occian   which on the desert lies—
There is a tribe   which never served our God—
You'll never hear   of any men more vile;
And they have hides   as hard as any iron,
So they care nothing   for hauberk or for helm.   3250
There are no soldiers   more savage in the realm.   AOI

CCXXXIV

Ten more divisions   the emir formed himself:
The first made up   of giants from Malprose,

3244. So Jenkins explains "Samuel's people," the Bulgars: "Under their
czar Samuel invaded the Eastern Roman Empire twenty-six times
between 988 and 1014."

The second, Huns; the third, Hungarians;
The fourth has men from Baldise la Longue;
The fifth has men who come from Val-Peneuse;
The sixth comes both from Inance and Marose;
The seventh: Leus and men of Styrmonis,
The eighth from Argoille, the ninth comes from Clarbonne,
3260 The tenth division: long-bearded men from Fronde—
⌐There is a tribe which has no love for God.
Thirty divisions the Chronicles count so.
Great are the hosts where those shrill trumpets play.
The pagans ride like heroes to the fray. AOI

CCXXXV

A mighty lord, the emir Baligant:
In front of him his dragon-standard goes,
And then a banner, the emblem of his gods;
There is an image of vile Apollo too.
Ten Canaanites on horseback ride around
3270 Shouting aloud this sermon as they go:
"All those who hope our gods will save them now,
Let them give heed: do penitence and pray!"
At that the pagans, bowing their heads and chins,
Bring their bright helmets down to the very ground.
The Frenchmen say, "Soon, felons, you shall die!
May utter ruin await you here today!
Heavenly Father, protect King Charlemagne,
And let this battle be given in his name!"

CCXXXVI

The great emir, experienced and wise,
3280 Calls to his presence his son and the two kings:
"My noble lords, your place is at the head
Of my divisions; you shall command them all,

3257. *Inance*, supplied by Jenkins.
3278. The meaning of this line is uncertain.

Except for three   that I'll keep in reserve:
One will be Turkish,   another Ormaleis,
And for the third,   the giants of Malprose.
The men of Occian   shall fight here at my side:
Those are the ones   who'll meet Charles and the French.
If Charlemagne   consents to fight with me,
There where his head is,   you'll see an empty space—
Thus will his rights   be honored by my grace!"   AOI   3290

CCXXXVII

Great are the hosts,   well ordered in brigades.
They see between them   no valley, hill or height,
No wood or forest   where ambush could be made:
They face each other   across a level plain.
Baligant says,   "My pagans, now's the time!
Mount up and ride—   our foes are on the field!"
The standard-bearer   is Amborre d'Oluferne;
As he goes by   they all shout "Précieuse!"
The Frenchmen answer,   "May this day be your last!"
And once again   their cry rings out: "Montjoie!"   3300
The Emperor Charles   has his clear trumpets sound,
And Roland's horn   which heartens all the Franks.
The pagans say,   "Charles has good men with him.
We'll have a battle   most terrible and grim."

CCXXXVIII

Wide is the field,   horizons far away.
The golden helmets,   set with fair jewels, gleam,
The ranks of shields,   the saffron-burnished mail,
And all the spears   with their bright flags of war.
The trumpets sound,   their voices clear and high;
The Oliphant   rings out above them all.   3310
Baligant summons   his brother to his side:
That's Canabeu,   the king of Floredée,
Who rules the land   as far as Val Sevrée.

The emir points   at Charlemagne's brigade:
"Look at the pride   of celebrated France!
With what fierce courage   the emperor sits his horse;
He's toward the rear   among those veterans
Who wear their hauberks   with their long beards outside,
White as the snow   when it lies over ice.
3320   They'll strike keen blows   with lances and with swords—
Stubborn and fierce   will be our battle here,
Greater than any   seen in the world before."
You couldn't throw   a well-peeled wand as far
As he rides on,   ahead of all his men.
Then with these words,   he urges them to fight:
"Pagans, come on!   and I will lead the way!"
He shakes his spear,   to make his meaning plain,
And holds it high,   the point toward Charlemagne. AOI

CCXXXIX

The Emperor Charles   looks at the great emir,
3330   His dragon-standard,   his banner and his flag,
The Arab forces   with their enormous hosts—
They've spread out over   the country on all sides,
Save for the land   he occupies himself.
Then Charlemagne   shouts in a mighty voice,
"Barons of France,   good vassals one and all!
You've fought and triumphed   in many hard campaigns!
Look at these pagans;   cowards they are, and vile!
The gods they worship   are not worth half a cent.
What does it matter   how many they may be?
3340   Let those men leave   who won't ride with me now!"
He digs his spurs   into his horse's side,
And Tencendur   leaps in the air four times.
"This is a valiant king,"   the Frenchmen say.
"Ride on, my lord,   we're with you, come what may!"

CCXL

Fair was the day,   the sun shone bright and clear.

The splendid hosts with their large companies
Move toward each other; the first are face to face.
Count Guinemant, and with him Count Rabel,
Let go their reins, send their swift horses on,
Spurring them hard. The warriors of France   3350
Gallop to strike with pointed spear and lance. AOI

CCXLI

A valiant knight, and strong, is Count Rabel.
He pricks his horse with spurs of shining gold,
Charges and strikes Torleu, the Persian king.
Hauberk and shield cannot withstand that blow:
Rabel's gold spear goes through him like a spit;
The king falls dead on top of a small bush.
The Frenchmen say, "Help us, almighty God!
Charles' cause is just; we must not fail him now." AOI

CCXLII

Guinemant charges Dapamort of the Wilzes,   3360
His first blow shatters the ornamented shield,
Then the king's hauberk goes flying into bits;
Up to the standard the spear has pierced his flesh;
Like it or not, the pagan king falls dead.
Seeing that blow, the men of France all shout,
"Now's the time, barons! Go to it, strike them down!
Against these pagans, the right is on Charles' side;
God sent us here to have this good cause tried!" AOI

CCXLIII

The prince, Malpramis, riding a pure white horse,
Forces his way right through the throng of Franks,   3370
Meeting each one with such prodigious blows
The dead pile up behind him as he goes.
And then rings out the voice of Baligant:
"Hear me, my barons, I've fed you for so long!

Look at my son,   he's hunting Charlemagne;
He wields his weapons   to challenge the French lords—
No better vassal   could any man desire.
Take up your spears!   Go out and help him now!"
Hearing these words,   the pagans charge the field;
3380   They strike hard blows   with all their might and main.
So wondrous fierce   the fighting grew, no war
Was ever like it,   since that time or before.   AOI

CCXLIV

Great are the hosts,   and proud their companies.
Now all divisions   are fighting on the field.
The pagan forces   strike with tremendous blows.
God! The spear shafts   splintered and cut in two,
The broken helmets,   the chain-mail split apart!
You would have seen them   like rushes on the ground.
The soft green grass   which covered all the field
3390   Was stained bright crimson   with French and pagan blood.
The emir speaks   to urge his household on:
"Strike hard, my lords;   let's cut these Christians down!"
No men have fought   so stubbornly and hard
Ever before,   or since, on any field;
Until the nightfall,   nothing will make them yield.   AOI

CCXLV

The great emir   calls out to all his men:
"Strike them down, pagans,   that's what you came here for!
I'll give you wives,   well-born and beautiful,
I'll give you fiefdoms,   wide lands and fair domains."
3400   The pagans answer,   "We'll do our part for that!"
Their mighty blows   have cost them all their spears;
They draw their swords,   a hundred thousand strong.
Then there's a slaughter,   a cruel, grim melee;
They see a battle,   those men who dare to stay!   AOI

3390. From V⁴.

CCXLVI

The Emperor Charles   then calls upon his Franks:
"I've faith in you, my lords;   I hold you dear
For all the battles   you've fought and won for me,
The kingdoms conquered,   the kings you've helped depose—
I don't forget   what recompense is due
From my own person,   and gifts of land and gold.   *3410*
Avenge your sons,   your brothers and your heirs—
Just yesterday   they died at Roncevaux!
Against the pagans   you know I'm in the right."
The French reply,   "My lord, you speak the truth."
The twenty thousand   that Charles has close to him
As with one voice   proclaim their loyalty:
They will not fail him   for suffering or death.
Each one of them   strikes with a spear or lance,
And after that   they'll fight on, sword in hand.
Grim war they wage   at Charlemagne's command. AOI   *3420*

CCXLVII

Prince Malpramis   rides through the battlefield,
And as he goes   he kills good men of France.
Naimon the Duke   watches with fiery eyes,
And then he charges,   the valiant chevalier;
His spear-point, passing   right through the upper shield,
Splits the gold border   where the chain-mail is joined.
Into the body   the yellow banner flies;
Malpramis falls   where seven hundred lie.

CCXLVIII

King Canabeu,   brother to the emir,
Urging his horse   with sharp pricks of the spur,   *3430*
Unsheathes his sword   which has a crystal hilt.
He'charges Naimon,   and strikes his tall gold helm;

Cracking wide upon,   the helmet breaks in two,
Five of the lacings   the steel blade slices through.
No one would give   two cents for that mail hood
Split by the sword   which reaches to the flesh—
Part of his scalp   is hurled down to the ground.
The duke is stunned   by that tremendous blow;
He would have fallen,   but for the help of God.
3440   He puts his arms   around his horse's neck,
And if that pagan   had charged him just once more,
The noble lord   would certainly have died.
But Charles of France   comes riding to his side. AOI

CCXLIX

Naimon the Duke   is in great need of help,
And Canabeu   hastens to strike again.
Charles says, "Vile serf,   you fought him to your woe!"
With mighty valor   he charges in and strikes;
He breaks the shield   against the pagan's heart,
The hauberk's neckpiece   yields to that fierce attack;
3450   An empty saddle   sits on the horse's back.

CCL

King Charlemagne   is overwhelmed with grief
When he sees Naimon   wounded before his eyes;
On the green grass   fall bright red drops of blood.
Then leaning toward him,   the emperor says this:
"Naimon, fair lord,   come ride beside me now!
That wretched serf   who threatened you is dead:
I took my spear   and ran him through and through."

3433. For *principale* Jenkins has "princely, magnificent."
3445. Here Bédier would have it that Canabeu was urging Charles to
strike, that is, egging him on. The alternate possibility, defended by
Jenkins, seems to me more probable. Canabeu's attention would
naturally be centered on Naimon, and Charlemagne's arrival would
only make Canabeu's own haste to strike the more urgent.

The duke replies, "My lord, I trust in you;
And if I live, this debt shall be repaid."
In loyal friendship they fight on side by side,   *3460*
With them the Franks, some twenty thousand men,
Wield sword or spear against the Saracens. AOI

CCLI

The great emir goes riding through the field;
He turns to charge, attacking Guinemant,
Whose shining shield is crushed against his heart.
The hauberk cracks, its panels split apart;
The spearhead crashes right through the Frenchman's chest;
The count is hurled from his swift-running horse.
Then the emir killed Geboin and Lorant,
Richard the Old, the lord of Normandy.   *3470*
The pagans say, "That is a valiant blade.
With Précieuse we cannot be afraid!" AOI

CCLII

You should have seen the knights of Araby,
Warriors of Occian, Blakia and Argoille!
Fiercely they strike, wielding their spears and swords,
And yet the French have no thought of retreat.
Not a few men on both sides fall and die.
The battle rages until the sky grows dark,
Great are the losses among the Frankish lords;
They'll see more grief before they end the war. AOI   *3480*

CCLIII

Both French and Arabs are striking wondrous blows,
Lances are shattered, and many burnished spears.
If you had been there when shields were smashed to bits,
If you had heard the hauberks meeting steel,
The sound of swords grating on top of helms!

If you had seen those valiant knights go down,
Screaming in anguish, dying there on the ground—
Then you would know what suffering can be!
This is a battle heavy and hard to bear.
3490 The emir prays, asking Apollo's help,
Invokes Mohammed, and Tervagant as well:
"Almighty gods, I've served you faithfully,
You shall have idols fashioned of purest gold!   AOI
I ask you now for triumph over Charles."
A favorite, Gemalfin, then comes forth
With woeful tidings he gives to the emir:
"Baligant, lord, this is an evil day:
For you have lost Malpramis, your fair son,
And Canabeu, your brother, has been slain.
3500· Of the two Franks who gained this victory,
I think that one was Charlemagne himself,
For he was tall and looked like a great lord,
His beard as white as any April flower."
Then the emir sits with his head bent down,
Under the helmet his face is stern and dark.
He feels he's dying, so bitterly he grieves;
He calls Jangleu, a man from overseas.

CCLIV

Says the emir, "Come forward now, Jangleu!
You have great courage, and you are very wise;
3510 I've always found your counsel to be true.
How do you see the Arabs and the French?
Are we to win the honors of this field?"
Jangleu replies, "Baligant, you are dead!
None of your gods will ever save you now.
King Charles is fierce, and valiant are the Franks—

3494. From V⁴.
3507. That is, Jangleu d'Outremer.
3510. Baligant's remark, a word of which is missing in the Oxford
manuscript, may mean that he has always followed Jangleu's advice.

I've never seen   such warlike men before.
But summon forth the Arabs,   the Occian lords,
Turks, Enfruns, Giants,   to help you while they may.
Whatever happens,   there's no good in delay."

CCLV

Outside his hauberk,   Baligant spreads his beard;   3520
The hawthorn flower   is not a purer white.
From what will come   he has no wish to hide.
Against his lips   he holds a clear-voiced horn,
And blows a call   which rings across the field;
The pagans, hearing,   rally their companies.
The men of Occian   start to whinny and bray,
The men of Argoille   are barking like great dogs;
They charge the Franks   with overwhelming force,
Splitting their ranks;   the French give way, fall back,
And seven thousand   are killed in that attack.   3530

CCLVI

Ogier, no man   to do a craven deed—
As good a knight   as ever put on mail—
Sees the French ranks   broken and split apart.
He summons Thierry,   the duke of the Argonne,
Geoffroy of Anjou,   and the Count Jozeran;
Then very fiercely   he speaks these words to Charles:
"See how the pagans   are killing off your men!
May God forbid   that your head wear a crown
If you won't strike   and so avenge your shame!"
No one replies,   no one will speak a word;   3540
Spurring their horses,   not to be left behind,
They charge to strike   whatever foes they find.   AOI

3526–7. This is not a pagan eccentricity, but the impression their languages made on the Christians.

CCLVII

Valiant in battle   are Charlemagne the King,
Naimon the Duke,   and Ogier the Dane,
Geoffroy of Anjou   who bore the flag for Charles.
There is a hero,   Count Ogier the Dane!
He spurs his horse   and gallops with all speed
To charge the pagan   who holds the dragon high,
Strikes at Amborre   who crashes to the ground,
3550   With him the dragon,   and the king's ensign too.
Baligant sees   the standard-bearer fall,
Mohammed's banner,   dishonored, come to grief;
Then the emir   begins to understand
That he is wrong,   and Charlemagne is right;
The Arab pagans   aren't making so much noise.
The Emperor Charles   calls out then to the Franks:
"Lords, will you help me?   I ask it in God's name."
The Franks reply,   "Why ask what you should know?
Cursed be the man   whose striking arm is slow!" AOI

CCLVIII

3560   The day goes by;   darkness begins to fall;
Pagans and Franks   are fighting with their swords.
Two men of courage   command these mighty hosts.
They don't forget   to sound their battle-calls,
The great emir   shouting his "Précieuse!"
And Charlemagne,   his famous cry "Montjoie!"
Each recognizes   the other's strong clear voice,
And then they meet   upon the battlefield.
They charge head on;   each one lands with his spear
So great a blow   upon the other's shield
3570   It cracks wide open   below the heavy boss;
The hauberk panels   are cracked and split apart,

3550. There are a dragon, an ensign, and possibly (3552) even a third
flag.
3555. The translation of this line derives from Jenkins' emendation.

And yet the spearheads   don't penetrate the flesh.
The girths give way,   throwing the saddles off,
With them both kings   come crashing to the ground.
Then, in an instant,   both have regained their feet
And drawn their swords,   ready to fight it out.
No way to end   this combat will be found
Till one of them   lies dead upon the ground.   AOI

CCLIX

A mighty hero   is Charlemagne of France,
And Baligant   will meet him unafraid.   3580
With swords unsheathed,   they come together now,
Their heavy shields   receiving mighty blows
Which split the leathers,   the double wooden frames;
The nails fall out,   the bosses break apart.
Then nothing shelters   the hauberks from the blades,
And fiery sparks   come flashing from their helms.
This is a combat   which has to last as long
As neither man   admits that he is wrong.   AOI

CCLX

Says the emir,   "Charles, if you stop and think,
You will repent   of what you've done to me: 3590
You can't deny   that you have killed my son;
You do great wrong   when you invade my lands.
Become my vassal,   promise me fealty;
Come with me to the East   and serve me there."
King Charles replies,   "That would be vile disgrace.
I'll be no friend   to pagans, or make peace.
Receive the law   that is the gift of God,
Become a Christian,   and you shall know my love;
Serve Him, have faith   in that almighty King."
Says Baligant,   "Tediously you preach!"   3600
They draw their swords,   and there's an end to speech.

CCLXI

The great emir   is powerful and brave:
He strikes Charles' helmet   so terrible a blow
The burnished steel   is cracked and splits apart,
The sword blade cleaves   the emperor's thick hair
And slices off   a hand's breadth of his scalp,
Stripping the flesh   down to the naked bone.
Charlemagne staggers,   comes close to falling down,
But God won't have him   brought to defeat or slain:
3610   Saint Gabriel   comes back to him once more,
And says, "Great king,   what are you waiting for?"

CCLXII

Charlemagne hears   the angel's holy voice:
He's not afraid,   he knows he will not die.
His strength returns,   his mind is clear and calm.
And then he strikes   with the great sword of France;
The emir's helmet,   ablaze with jewels, cracks,
His head is broken   so that the brains spill out,
His face splits open   down to his long white beard:
He is stone dead   before he hits the ground.
3620   Then Charles' "Montjoie!"   rings through the battlefield.
Duke Naimon hears him   and hastens to his side
With Tencendur;   the great king mounts his horse.
Now by God's will,   the pagans turn and flee;
The Frenchmen know   they've won their victory.

CCLXIII

The pagans flee,   for that is what God wills,
The Franks, with Charles,   are riding in pursuit.
The emperor says,   "My lords, avenge your grief,

3611. *Reis magnes, que fais tu?*—"Great king, what are you doing?"

Relieve your anger   and you will cheer your hearts;
I saw this morning   how tears flowed from your eyes."
They answer, "Sire,   that is what we must do."   3630
So many pagans   the Franks cut down and slay
That very few   manage to get away.

CCLXIV

The day is hot,   the air is thick with dust;
The pagans flee,   still harried by the Franks:
To Saragossa   they chase them all the way.
Queen Bramimonde   has gone up to her tower;
With her are clerics,   the priesthood of her faith,
That false religion   for which God has no love:
They're not ordained,   nor have they tonsured heads.
She sees the Arabs   running in wild retreat,   3640
And cries aloud,   "Mohammed, help us now!
Alas, fair king,   our men have fled the field,
The great emir,   dishonored, has been slain!"
When Marsile hears her,   he turns to face the wall,
Tears fill his eyes,   he lets his head sink down;
He dies of grief   that nothing can console,
And to quick demons   yields up his sinful soul. AOI

CCLXV

Dead are the pagans,   except for those who fled,
And Charlemagne   is master of the field.
In Saragossa   the gate is beaten down,   3650
There's no one left   who will defend it now.
Charles takes the stronghold;   his people come inside;
By right of conquest   they sleep there that same night.
Proud is the king   whose beard is silver-grey!
And Bramimonde   has yielded all the towers,

3648. *Alquant turnet en fuie* from V⁴.

Ten that are large   and fifty that are small.
He does great things   who on God's aid can call!

CCLXVI

The day is over;   now in the dark of night
The moon shines clear,   and stars flame in the sky.
3660   All Saragossa   belongs to Charlemagne.
A thousand Frenchmen   go searching through the town,
Through mosques and temples   of pagan infidels;
With iron hammers   and wedges in their hands
They break the idols,   and all the images,
Putting an end   to magic sorcery.
The king loves God,   and wants to serve Him well;
Calling his bishops,   he has the water blessed,
And then the pagans   are brought to be baptized.
If there are any   who still resist King Charles,
3670   He has them hanged,   or killed by fire or sword.
A hundred thousand   and a good many more
Are baptized Christians;   only the queen is left.
She will be taken,   a captive, to sweet France
To be converted   by love, as Charles commands.

CCLXVII

The night has passed;   when the bright day appears,
Charles leaves a guard   in Saragossa's towers:
A thousand of his knights   remain behind
To hold the city   in the emperor's name.
The king rides on   with all his other men
3680   And Bramimonde   he holds against her will—
But Charles desires   only to do her good.
In joy and triumph   the Frenchmen leave for home;
They seize Nerbone,   continue on their way,
And when they reach   Saint Seurin's in Bordeaux,
Charles stops to leave   upon the alter there
The Oliphant,   filled up with gold and coins,

As all the pilgrims who pass that way can see.
Finding large boats, for crossing the Gironde,
King Charles escorts his nephew into Blaye,
And his companion, the noble Oliver,   3690
And the Archbishop, so valiant and so wise.
In white stone coffins Charles has the three lords placed;
In Saint-Romain the noble barons lie.
The Franks commend them to God and to His names.
Charlemagne rides through valleys, over hills—
He will not stop until he reaches Aix;
There he draws rein beside the mounting block.
From his high palace the emperor sends out
His messengers to judges of his court:
Saxons, Bavarians, Frisians, men of Lorraine,   3700
To Alemans and men of Burgundy,
And Poitevins, Normans and Bretons too,
Frenchmen whose wisdom Charles can rely upon.
And now begins the trial of Ganelon.

CCLXVIII

The Emperor Charles has now returned from Spain.
He comes to Aix, his capital in France,
Enters the palace and goes to the great hall.
Alda, a lovely maiden, comes to him there.
She asks the king: "Where is the chieftain count,
Roland, who swore that I would be his wife?"   3710
Charles, as she speaks, is overcome with grief;
Tears fill his eyes, he pulls at his white beard:
"Sister, sweet friend, I can't bring back the dead.
But I will give you one better in his place.
You'll marry Louis— that's all that I can do—
He is my son, and he shall rule my realm."
Alda replies, "Your words seem to me strange.
The saints and angels, and God above forbid

3694. There were prayers containing long lists of the various names
of God.

That I live on   when Roland has been slain!"
3720   Her color fades,   she falls down at Charles' feet,
And dies—may God   have mercy on her soul!
The lords of France   mourn her and weep for woe.

CCLXIX

Alda the fair   has taken leave of life.
Charlemagne thinks   that she has only swooned;
The emperor feels   such pity that he weeps.
He takes her hands,   and draws her to her feet;
Upon her shoulder   her head hangs limply down.
Charles understands   that she is really dead.
He summons then   four noble countesses,
3730   Has Alda's body   borne to a nunnery;
There they keep vigil   all night until the dawn.
Beside the altar   she has an honored grave,
Richly endowed   by will of Charlemagne. AOI

CCLXX

The Emperor Charles   has come back home to Aix.
There Ganelon,   the traitor, bound with chains,
In the high town,   before the palace stands.
To a great stake   the serfs have bound him fast,
Both of his hands   are tied with deerskin thongs,
They beat him well   with heavy sticks and rods:
3740   That way he's treated   in the most proper style,
And he must wait   in torment for his trial.

CCLXXI

As it is written   in the old chronicles,
Charlemagne summoned   vassals from many lands;
And in the chapel   at Aix they're gathered now.
The day is solemn,   the feast they celebrate
Is Saint Silvester's—   so many people say.

The trial begins   with speeches on both sides,
And Ganelon,   who did a traitor's deed,
Is dragged before   the emperor to plead.   AOI

CCLXXII

"Barons, my lords,"   says Charlemagne the king,   3750
"Give me your judgment   concerning Ganelon.
He was with me in Spain   among my host,
And there he robbed me   of twenty thousand Franks;
My nephew Roland   you'll never see again,
Nor Oliver,   so courteous and brave—
For gold and treasure   this man betrayed the peers."
"Sire," says the count,   "I won't conceal the truth:
Because of Roland   I lost both goods and gold.
I wanted him   to suffer and to die;
But in that vengeance   there was no treachery."   3760
The Franks reply,   "We'll talk of this and see."

CCLXXIII

Before the king   behold Count Ganelon.
Stalwart he stands,   fair color in his face—
If he were loyal,   he'd look a noble lord.
He sees the French,   the judges who are there,
The thirty members   of his own family,
And then he speaks,   his great voice ringing out:
"Barons of France,   for God's sake hear me now!
My lords, I fought   beside the emperor,
And served him well   in loyalty and love.   3770
His nephew Roland,   hating me in his heart,
Had me condemned   to torment and sure death:
I was to bring   Charles' message to Marsile—
I had the wit   and wisdom to survive.
I faced Count Roland   and challenged him aloud,
And Oliver,   and all the other peers.
Charlemagne heard me,   so did these noble lords:

I am avenged, but not by treachery."
The Franks reply, "We'll go and judge your plea."

CCLXXIV

3780   Ganelon sees his great trial has begun.
Thirty kinsmen the count has with him there,
Among them one looked up to by the rest
Called Pinabel— his castle is Sorence.
This man can argue so that his views prevail,
And he's a hero not easy to defeat. AOI
Ganelon says, "I place my trust in you—
Save me from death, defend me in this trial!"
Says Pinabel, "In no time you'll be free.
If any Frenchman decides that you should hang,
3790   The Emperor Charles must have that judgment tried:
My sword shall prove these accusations lies."
Count Ganelon with grateful thanks replies.

CCLXXV

Bavarians, Saxons, have gone to judge the case,
Normans are with them, Poitevins, men of France,
Germans are there, and many Thiois too;
Those from Auvergne show the most courtesy.
They speak more softly because of Pinabel,
Telling each other, "Let's bring this to an end,
Dismiss the trial, and ask that Charles the King
3800   For this one time let Ganelon go free—
He'll be his vassal in loyalty and love.
Roland is dead; you won't see him again.
No gold or treasure will bring him back to life.

3786. The line is defective in the Oxford manuscript; thus Jenkins.
3792. It is probable that Ganelon did not literally fall at Pinabel's feet,
as a literal translation would indicate.
3796. But Jenkins translates corteis as "compassionate," and says it may
also mean "skilled in the law."

It would be madness   to fight for his sake now."
They all approve;   no one will disagree
But Geoffroy's brother,   the chevalier Thierry.   AOI

CCLXXVI

And so the barons   return to Charlemagne,
Saying to him,   "Sire, we would ask for this:
Acquit your captive,   let Ganelon go free,
Henceforth to serve you   loyally and with love.
Grant him his life,   for he is nobly born;
And no man's death   will bring Count Roland back,
Nor any gold—   there's nothing to be done."
Then says the king,   "You're traitors, every one!"   AOI

3810

CCLXXVII

When King Charles sees   they all have failed his cause,
He bows his head   so none can see his face;
His words and looks   proclaim his bitter woe.
And then before him   he sees a chevalier,
Thierry, whose brother   is Geoffroy of Anjou.
Not very stalwart,   he's lean and spare of build,
His hair is black,   his face is rather dark;
He isn't tall,   nor could you call him short.
With courtesy   he tells the emperor:
"Fair sire and king,   do not give way to grief!
You know I've served you   a long time faithfully.
Now all my forebears   through me protest this trial:
However Roland   may have wronged Ganelon,
No one may harm   a man who serves the king.

3820

3812. The translation here follows Jenkins' interpretation of *ja por morir*,
but his substitution of *getun* for *gerun* ("No matter who dies, we'll
never see a son of Roland's") seems extravagant.
3820. The point is that Thierry will really need God's help if he is to
prevail against Pinabel; thus the case will be better proved. And when
he does win, the Franks immediately shout, "A holy miracle!" (3931).

3830

Count Ganelon   is thus a traitor proved;
His oath to you   was broken and betrayed.
And so I judge   that he should hang and die,
And that his body   be treated as befits
A criminal   who's guilty of a crime.
If he has kinsmen   who'd argue this with me,
I'll use this sword   girded here at my side
To give my judgment   a prompt and sure defense."
The Franks reply,   "Your argument makes sense."

CCLXXVIII

3840

Now Pinabel   stands up before the king;
He's tall and strong,   valiant and very swift:
The man he strikes   won't see another day.
He says to Charles,   "Sire, you convoked this trial;
Pray, then, keep order—   let's not have so much noise.
And as for Thierry,   his judgment has been heard.
I say he's wrong—   now let him come and fight."
His right-hand glove   he offers to the king.
The emperor says,   "I ask for hostages."
His thirty kinsmen   will sponsor Pinabel.
Says Charlemagne,   "He's free then, in your place."
They will be guarded   till justice ends the case. AOI

CCLXXIX

3850

When Thierry sees   that Pinabel will fight,
He gives his glove,   the right one, to the king,
And Charlemagne,   his hostage, sets him free.
Charles has four benches   arranged to mark the field;
Those who will fight   go out to take their seats.

3845. The glove, as in line 2839, symbolizes the fief, given now to the
king, his overlord, to whom it will revert in case the vassal is killed.
Similarly in line 2851.
3852. It seems, but is not certain, that Charles himself acted as hostage
for Thierry.

All think the challenge   well given, rightly met;
Ogier explains   how they are to proceed.
Horses and arms   are sent for with all speed.

CCLXXX

The knights are ready   to meet for their ordeal.   AOI
They've made confession,   have been absolved and blessed,
They've heard a mass,   taken communion too;   *3860*
Great offerings   they've given to the church.
Now when the champions   appear before the king,
They both are wearing   sharp spurs upon their feet,
They've put on hauberks,   shining and light and strong,
Their burnished helmets   are closed around their heads,
They gird on swords   whose hilts are of pure gold.
Around their necks   they hang their quartered shields,
Their right hands grasp   the long sharp-pointed spears.
Now they have mounted   war-horses bred for speed.
Seeing them go,   a hundred thousand knights   *3870*
Remember Roland   and weep for Thierry—
For God knows what   the end of this will be!

CCLXXXI

In a broad meadow   below Aix la Chapelle,
The barons meet;   their battle has begun.
Both are courageous,   both of them valiant lords,
And their war-horses   are spirited and swift.
They spur them hard,   and loosening the reins,
They charge each other   and strike with all their might.
Both shields are shattered—   they're broken into bits—
The hauberks break,   the girths are split apart,   *3880*
The saddles fall,   and with them both the knights.
A hundred thousand   are weeping at the sight.

3856. This is Jenkins' interpretation of *purparlet*, similar to that in
Bédier's glossary, although different from his translation.

CCLXXXII

Both chevaliers   have fallen to the ground.   AOI
Losing no time,   they're on their feet again.
Agile and swift   is Pinabel, and strong;
They face each other—   they have no horses now—
And raise their swords   whose hilts are made of gold
To strike and hew   each other's shining helms;
Those heavy blows   can cut right through the steel.
3890   The French lament,   thinking their man must fail.
"O God," says Charles,   "now let the right prevail!"

CCLXXXIII

Says Pinabel,   "Thierry, admit you've lost!
I'll be your vassal   in loyalty and love,
All I possess   shall be at your command—
But reconcile   the king and Ganelon."
Then Thierry answers,   "That's easy to decide!
I'll take no offer   unworthy of a knight!
Let God determine   which one of us is right!"   AOI

CCLXXXIV

And Thierry says,   "Pinabel, you are brave;
3900   You're tall and strong,   your body is well built,
That you are valiant   is known to all your peers.
This is a battle   you can afford to lose!
I'll make your peace   with Charlemagne the king,
But Ganelon   must get what he deserves—
No day will pass   without his death retold."
Says Pinabel,   "Almighty God forbid!
I stand here now   for all my family—
I won't surrender   to any man on earth!
Better to die   than live to merit blame."
3910   So once again   they slash with their great swords,

Striking the helmets   brilliant with gold and jewels—
Great fiery sparks   fly out against the sky.
Now neither champion   will to the other yield
Until a dead man   is lying on the field.   AOI

CCLXXXV

He's a strong fighter,   Pinabel of Sorence,
The blow he strikes   on Thierry's burnished helm
Sends out such sparks   the grass is set on fire.
Then he springs forward,   the point of his steel blade
Cutting right through   from Thierry's forehead down;
Along his face   the sword point slashes deep,   3920
And blood springs out   all over his right cheek;
Down to his waist   the hauberk links all tear—
Without God's help,   he'd have died then and there!   AOI

CCLXXXVI

When Thierry sees   he's wounded in the face,
His bright blood falling   over the meadow grass,
Pinabel's helmet   of burnished steel he strikes:
Down through the nose-piece   it cracks and splits in two,
His skull is broken   and spills the brains inside;
With one last flourish   Thierry has felled him dead—
With that great blow   he's master of the field.   3930
The Frenchmen shout,   "A holy miracle!
Justice demands   that Ganelon must die,
With all the kinsmen   who came and took his side."   AOI

CCLXXXVII

Thierry has won   his triumph on the field.
The Emperor Charles   comes out to give him thanks;
Four of his barons   attend the emperor:
Naimon the Duke,   Count Ogier the Dane,
William of Blaye   and Geoffroy of Anjou.

3932. Up to and including this line, it has always been assumed that
Ganelon would be hanged.

King Charlemagne   takes Thierry in his arms,
3940 And wipes his face   with royal marten furs;
These he puts down—   they bring another cloak.
Thierry's armor   is gently taken off;
Charles has him mounted   on an Arabian mule.
Most joyfully   they bring the hero home;
They come to Aix   and in the square dismount.
Now they will kill   the kinsmen of the count.

CCLXXXVIII

Charlemagne summons   the nobles of his court:
"What do you counsel   about my hostages?
These men came here   to plead for Ganelon,
3950 And stayed as pledges,   sponsoring Pinabel."
The Franks reply,   "Ill work if one survives!"
The king commands   an officer, Basbrun:
"Go hang them all   upon the gallows tree!
And by my beard   whose hair is silver-grey,
If one escapes,   you're dead and put to shame."
The man replies,   "I'll do as you command."
A hundred servants   help him to drag them off;
They hang all thirty   that they were told to take.
So one man's evil   draws others in its wake. AOI

CCLXXXIX

3960 They all agree: Bavarians, Alemans,
Poitevins, Bretons,   and men from Normandy,
And first of all   the Franks who come from France,
That Ganelon   should die most horribly.
And so they order   four war-horses brought out
To which they tie   Ganelon's feet and hands.
These are proud chargers,   spirited, bred for speed:
Four servants urge them   the way they ought to go.
There where a river   across a meadow flows,

Count Ganelon   is utterly destroyed:
His ligaments   are twisted and stretched out,   3970
His every limb   is cracked and splits apart;
On the green grass   the bright blood runs in streams.
So Ganelon   as a foul traitor died.
Let no man's treason   give comfort to his pride!

CCXC

The Emperor Charles, his vengeance being done,
Summoned his bishops,   the ones who came from France,
Bavarians   and Alemans as well:
"A noble captive   is dwelling in this house;
She's heard such sermons   and edifying tales,
She trusts in God,   and wants to take the Faith.   3980
Baptize her now,   that God may have her soul."
The bishops answer,   "Let godmothers be found!"
. . . .
A great assembly   was gathered at the baths
To see the Queen of Spain   receive the Faith;
To Juliana   they now have changed her name.
She had true knowledge   when Christian she became.

CCXCI

The Emperor Charles,   once justice has been done,
And his great anger   is finally appeased,   3990
Has Bramimonde   baptized into the Faith.
The day is over,   and in the dark of night
The king lies sleeping   in his high vaulted room.
Saint Gabriel   is sent by God to say:

3983. Part of a word is missing from this line which Bédier leaves
blank. It apparently described the godmothers as "trustworthy and
good-looking" (Jenkins) or "pious and of noble lineage" (Mortier).
3984. The missing word here begins with c, and compaignes (Jenkins)
seems likely.

"Charlemagne, summon   your empire's mighty hosts!
You'll march in force   into the land of Bire;
You must relieve   King Vivien at Imphe
Where pagans hold   his city under siege,
And Christian voices   are crying for your help."
The Emperor Charles   has no desire to go.
4000 "God!" says the king,   "how weary is my life!"
He pulls his beard,   the tears flow from his eyes.
Here ends the poem,   for Turoldus declines.

3995–6. Nothing is known of Bire, Imphe, or Vivien except that they
were all Christian.
4002. The ending of the poem, *Ci falt la geste que Turoldus declinet*, is
very famous for being so enigmatic. *Que* may mean either "which" or
"because" (Jenkins); *declinet* may mean "to compose, sing, recite, or
copy." It may also mean to "set," as the sun sets, or to become infirm.
While it is true that my version favors the idea of the poet's explaining
why he does not continue his work with Charlemagne's new expedition,
the reason for this disinclination is left as imprecise as possible. I hoped
mainly to let the poem end with the same frustrating vagueness as
does the original.

The Library of Liberal Arts

SCHILLER, J., Wilhelm Tell

SCHLEGEL, J., On Imitation and
Other Essays

SCHNEIDER, H., Sources of
Contemporary
Philosophical Realism
in America

SCHOPENHAUER, A., On the Basis
of Morality
Freedom of the Will

SELBY-BIGGE, L., British Moralists

SENECA, Medea
Oedipus
Thyestes

SHAFTESBURY, A., Characteristics

SHELLEY, P., A Defence of Poetry

SMITH, A., The Wealth of Nations
(Selections)

Song of Roland, Terry, trans.

SOPHOCLES, Electra

SPIEGELBERG, H., The Socratic
Enigma

SPINOZA, B., Earlier Philosophic
Writings
On the Improvement of the
Understanding

TERENCE, The Brothers
The Eunuch
The Mother-in-Law
Phormio
The Self-Tormentor
The Woman of Andros

Three Greek Romances, Hadas,
trans.

TOLSTOY, L., What is Art?

VERGIL, Aeneid

VICO, G. B., On the Study Method
Our Time

VOLTAIRE, Philosophical Letters

WHITEHEAD, A., Interpretation of
Science

WOLFF, C., Preliminary Discour
on Philosophy in Gener

XENOPHON, Recollections of
Socrates *and* Socrates'
Defense Before the Jur